A SOCIAL LEARNING APPROACH TO FAMILY INTERVENTION

VOLUME 2:

Observation in Home Settings

edited by
John B. Reid

A SOCIAL LEARNING APPROACH TO FAMILY INTERVENTION

VOLUME 2:

Observation in Home Settings

edited by
John B. Reid

Oregon Social Learning Center

Castalia Publishing Company
P.O. Box 1587
Eugene, Oregon 97440

Copyright © 1978 by Castalia Publishing Company

All rights reserved. No part of this book may be reproduced by mimeograph, xerox, or any other means without the written permission of the publisher. Excerpts may be printed in connection with published reviews in periodicals without express permission. Printed in the United States of America.

Library of Congress Catalog Card Number: 77-928-35

ISBN: 0-916154-01-7

Copies of this book may be ordered from the publisher.

Cover photo by Craig S. Patterson

Dedication

This book is dedicated to Betty Brummett, Rachel Condon, LaVella Garber, and Jonnie Johnson without whose efforts the present code would not have been developed.

TABLE OF CONTENTS

Editor's Notes and Acknowledgments   IX

Chapter 1   1
Observation as a Mode of Investigation
G.R. Patterson and S.L. Maerov

Chapter 2   3
Development of the Family Interaction Coding System (FICS)
G.R. Patterson, J.B. Reid, & S.L. Maerov

Chapter 3   11
The Observation System: Methodological Issues and Psychometric Properties
G.R. Patterson, J.B. Reid, & S.L. Maerov

Chapter 4   21
Coding of Family Interactions
S.L. Maerov, B. Brummett, G.R. Patterson, and J.B. Reid

Chapter 5   37
Observer Training
S.L. Maerov, B. Brummett, & J.B. Reid

Chapter 6   43
The Development of Specialized Observational Systems
J.B. Reid

References   51

Appendices   59

Editor's Note

Observational data has been the foundation of our clinical and theoretical work for the last decade. Not only have we utilized the present system for evaluating the outcome of our treatment, but also as a mechanism for providing therapists with continuous and concrete feedback on their work with individual clients.

This book represents an attempt to describe the problems involved in the collection of home observation data and our solutions to those problems. A chapter has been included to explain the process of devising and evaluating an observational coding system which is tailor-made to meet specialized needs. This manual is designed for use by both students of psychology and human ecology, as well as for the behavioral scientist who wishes to apply our omnibus coding system in home settings.

Although I am the editor of this volume, I am by no stretch of the imagination the sole author of the present system. It had its beginnings in my dissertation research under Dr. Gerald R. Patterson, and has developed in collaboration with him and the other authors of this volume. The work began in 1966 at the University of Oregon and was extended at Oregon Research Institue. Our work on observational systems is now being conducted at a new and exciting site — the Oregon Social Learning Center, an affiliate of the Wright Institute of Berkeley, California.

John B. Reid

Acknowledgments

The following persons contributed in a significant way to the completion of this manual: J. Arnold, B. Brummett, W. Carlson, P. Chamberlain, J. Cobb, R. Condon, B. Conger, B. Danaher, V. Devine, M. Dumaresq, M. Forgatch, L. Garber, A. Harris, N. Hawkins, H. Hops, J. Johnson, R. Jones, D. Leslie, S. Maerov, G. Patterson, R. Ray, J. Reid, K. Reid, B. Sanson-Fisher, D. Shaw, K. Skindrud, M. Weinrott, G. White, T. Wills, and N. Wiltz.

Chapter 1

Observation as a Mode of Investigation

**G.R. Patterson
and S.L. Maerov**

The data collection system described in this book evolved in response to a need for an assessment methodology which could measure changes in family interactions. The observational system was designed to fulfill these tasks: (a) to provide data for the continuous monitoring of clinical cases; (b) to provide data for the systematic assessment of family intervention outcome; and (c) to provide a data base upon which to develop a theory of how aggressive behavior might be acquired and maintained within a family.

Reviews of early applications of observation methodologies with children (e.g., Wright, 1960) reflect a narrow conception of the scope and scientific usefulness of such observations. Not only were early observational studies limited primarily to preschool subjects, but the settings sampled were, for the most part, restricted to the nursery school. In addition, the observational systems provided only crude data such as simple frequency counts of molar behaviors (e.g., Olson, 1930), or judgments of trait behaviors (e.g., Goodenough, 1930). As Wright (1960) pointed out, such gross descriptive data simply did not allow for precise hypotheses testing. In fact, these early studies generated few hypotheses about children's social behaviors. The main contributions of early observational investigations were their sophisticated studies of the psychometric problems involved in the collection of observation data. Analyses by Thomas, Loomis, and Arrington (1933) of observer reliability, stability of event sampling, and observer error were models in this regard. Although crude by today's standards, the data collected in these early studies merit closer study than they have received. Some of the findings relate to current issues and theories. For example, an incidental finding reported by Goodenough (1930) showed that situational changes produced differential effects on the behavior of different subjects.

Aside from the area of child psychology, early work on the development of observation techniques was astonishingly lacking in sophistication regarding measurement problems inherent in the collection of observation data. This is reflected in a review by Heyns and Lippitt (1954) in which it is pointed out that problems of event sampling, observer presence effects, observer bias, observer drift, sequential dependencies, and validity had hardly been considered, much less investigated. Certainly, the generation of investigators trained during the 50's and 60's in the complex problems of response bias, social desirability, test/retest reliability, internal reliability, itemetrics, and construct validity could hardly be expected to take seriously a branch of science that ignored these realities. As suggested in recent reviews of observation techniques by Wiggins (1973b), Johnson and Bolstad (1973), and Jones, Reid, and Patterson (1975), *all* of the traditional psychometric puzzles are to be found within the observation methodologies. Jones (1973) suggests that there are, in fact, additional problems raised by observation methodologies for which traditional assessment literature has no answers.

A new look in observation methodology was provided by Roger Barker and his colleagues in the early 1950's (e.g., Barker, 1951; Barker, 1968; Barker & Wright, 1954; Willems & Rausch, 1969). Rather than concentrating solely on the subject, Barker's group devised methodology focused upon the sampling of the *environment as it interacted with the child*. In the two and a half decades following the publication of Barker's *One Boy's Day* (1951), data were collected over a broad range of settings in both the USA and England. The range of subjects and behaviors were expanded far beyond the limits of the nursery school classroom. Hypotheses were being tested *and* generated to the extent that by the mid-1950's reviews of observation literature were more optomistic about the utility of this approach. Recent reviews (Johnson & Bolstad, 1973; Jones *et al.*, 1975; Lytten, 1971; Weick, 1968) reflect the solid empirical basis of the recent developments in methodology. These reviews also emphasize the collection of sequentially ordered rather than simple frequency or summary data.

Barker and his group emphasized the collection of data relating to such macro units as Behavior Episodes, Behavioral Settings, and Environmental Force Units. Observation data were collected in narrative form. It was assumed that discrete units of "behavior" occurred in nature and could be identified by examining these narrative accounts. The large number of hypotheses tested by these data attest to the power of this approach. However, the omnibus narrative recording procedure refined by the Barker group did not produce data of sufficient specificity to allow for the intensive study of molecular social events.

Recent observational studies (e.g., Bobbitt, Gourevitch, Miller, & Jenson, 1969; Caldwell, 1971; Patterson, Ray, Shaw, & Cobb, 1969) differ from the pioneering efforts of Barker and his colleagues. Rather than stressing exhaustive narrative reports of interaction, the emphasis is on tailoring the code systems to test hypotheses about limited aspects of behavior. Rather than simply analyzing event frequencies, behavior is examined for inter-dependencies with environmental events. The theories which emerge are interaction theories. Each social behavior requires the construction of its own tailor-made coding device. In the Family Interaction Coding System (FICS), the code primarily samples coercive behaviors used among family members. The data lend themselves to the analyses of changes in rates of behaviors which are of clinical interest. They also lend themselves to yet more complex units such as the frequency with which a parent responds punitively to a specific kind of child behavior (e.g., Taplin & Reid, 1976). Of even greater interest are the data showing changes in dyad members as a function of extended interaction chains (e.g., Patterson, 1974c).

Ultimately, the utility of this molecular approach rests on the precision of the measuring device. The process of analyzing and altering the device continues to be an integral part of the research at the Oregon Social Learning Center. The description of the studies which follow in the next two sections summarize the status of this research up to 1977.

Chapter 2

Development of the Family Interaction Coding System [FICS]

**G.R. Patterson,
J.B. Reid, and S.L. Maerov**

Our approach to family therapy places particular stress upon the continuing need for *change* in intervention procedures (Patterson, Reid, Jones, & Conger, 1975). The reason for this emphasis lies in the fact that the best existing procedures meet only the minimal requirements for effective treatment of problem children. Although outcome studies have shown that many severely aggressive children can be helped by the present procedures (Patterson, 1974a, 1974b, 1975; Reid & Patterson, 1976), a significant minority realize no measurable benefits. In addition, two follow-up studies suggest that some parents slip back or retain many of their earlier modes of interacting with their children (Patterson, 1976; Taplin & Reid, 1976). Although a perfectly effective treatment for aggressive children will never be attained, the odds for therapeutic success can always be improved if treatment procedures are continuously modified on the basis of outcome effectiveness.

The genuine possibility of constantly improving therapy practices comes not from the therapist's good intentions, but rather from the therapist's use of frequent inputs of relatively high quality data. This contingency arrangement requires that the therapist receive at least weekly assessments of the behavior of the child, and perhaps of his own therapeutic behavior as well. Given feedback of reasonably reliable and valid data, then the therapist is in a position to continuously *change his own behavior* to achieve optimal effectiveness. Over time, favored techniques which are not supported by the data must be discarded. The void created by discarded techniques must be filled by new innovations which in turn will be evaluated. Over time, one would expect the treatment procedures not only to look different, but also to become increasingly useful.

Therapists in traditional treatment settings have almost always received verbal feedback from parents and sometimes from teachers. However, the reviews of child therapy studies by Levitt (1957, 1971) suggest that over a period of two decades, there have been *no* increases in the efficiency of traditional therapies being applied by well-trained personnel. The present writers assume that this impasse occurs because the feedback data given to therapists have been consistently biased. The bias is a relatively consistent tendency on the part of parents of disturbed children to report improvement in the behavior of their child when in fact no real changes have occured. Data reviewed in the section which follows suggest that roughly two-thirds of such parents will report improvements when asked for global judgments. This means that even if the therapy *isn't working*, the therapist will receive supportive comments from the *majority* of the families with which he works. Given such reinforcement, there is, of course, little reason for the therapist to change his behavior.

Reliability and Validity of Parent Global Report Data

The following is a review of the research pertaining to three different types of parents' *global* judgments: (a) parents' descriptions of child-rearing practices, (b) parents' descriptions of their child's behavior, and (c) parents' reports of changes in deviant behavior. In this context, the term global refers to attempts by parents to synthesize information from extended time periods (e.g., more than 24 hours) and/or covering a range of broad-spectrum variables which are defined only by conventional useage (e.g., such terms as "warmth," or "destructive"). Such global judgments have typically been made in the *absence of prior systematic observations* by the parent.

Child-rearing

One commonly used method for obtaining data from the parent is the clinical interview. In some instances, the parent uses rating scales to make judgments of the child's adjustment. In other cases, the interviewer summarizes the information provided by parents. Regardless of format, there are studies which suggest that the different interviewers obtain very different information from parents, and that the same interviewers receive different information from parents from one interview to the next (e.g., Mcfarlene, Allen, & Honzik, 1962).

Much research on socialization has been based upon parents' recollection of childrearing patterns. The reliability of such recall, however, has been called repeatedly into question (e.g., Robins, 1963; Yarrow, Campbell, & Burton, 1964, 1970). These data which show that parents are not always accurate in reporting information about their children raises doubt about the utility of intensive efforts to get developmental histories using traditional child guidance interview procedures.

The validity of parent global ratings has also been checked by comparing such ratings with reports from the child, school records, and systematic observations. In one study (Burton, 1970), mothers' judgments and school records showed low correlations. A study by Schelle (1974) showed *no* correlation between *changes* in school attendance reported in school files and parent reports. Burton (1970) reported little convergence between parent and child judgments about trait measures describing the child. This finding is consistent with the low level of agreement (40%–60%) between parent and child for even relatively well-specified symptoms such as fears, overactivity, and temper tantrums found by Lapouse and Monk (1958).

This lack of support for the validity of parents' global judgments is also found in studies using observation procedures as a criterion measure. These studies show only low level correlations between ratings based upon interviews with the mother and observations of mother/child interaction (e.g., Antonovsky, 1959). Many of our "facts" concerning the functional relationships between mothers and children may be determined primarily by the method of data collection, e.g., interview versus observation (Bing, 1963). Although some studies show modest agreement for molar variables across methods (e.g., Smith, 1958), the majority of studies show discontinuities (e.g., Baumrind & Black, 1967; Burton, 1970; Honig, Tannenbaum, & Caldwell, 1968; Sears, 1965).

In examining the problem further, it seems that persons living within the same system do not necessarily agree in their global perceptions of child behavior. Mothers' and fathers' trait ratings of their children show only modest positive correlations (Becker, 1960). Similarly, Novick, Rosenfeld, and Block (1965) showed only 36% agreement between parents in identifying problem behaviors in their own child. The conclusion to be drawn from these studies is that parents are unable to provide reliable or valid global reports of their children's behavior.

Therapy change

Here again, parents' global judgments prove to be of questionable validity. Several studies have suggested that parents have a bias to report improvement in the behavior of problem children when no observable changes have occurred. This is of some importance because of Levitt's (1957, 1971) claim that better than two-thirds of *non*-treated emotionally disturbed children improve over time. His reviews were based upon studies which used parent report as the primary outcome criterion. Given the presence of parental bias, then, his estimates for base rates of spontaneous change would seem considerably inflated.

In a study by Collins (1966), the treatment of children with problems had been delayed and it was therefore necessary to re-establish a baseline measure of adjustment. The parents did not know of this situation. When asked for new ratings of their children, they assumed the children had been receiving treatment. Their ratings showed significant improvement, even though treatment had *not* yet begun. A similar finding was obtained for a no-treatment control condition in a study by Clement and Milne (1967). It is possible that the children's behavior improved simply as a function of the passage of time. However, the findings also support the hypothesis that parents perceived change when none, in fact, occurred.

A study reported by Walter and Gilmore (1973) showed that parents' global ratings of changes were unrelated to the actual behavior of the child. In that study, families were randomly assigned to experimental and placebo groups. Multiple criterion data were collected during baseline and again five weeks later to assess changes in child behavior. Observation data were collected in the homes. In addition, each parent, during baseline and intervention, made daily reports on the occurrence/non-occurrence of a list of behaviors for which they had come for assistance. Both sets of criterion data showed significant decreases in observed rates of targeted deviant behaviors for families in the experimental group. There was a non-significant *increase* in rates for the families in the placebo group. However, parents' global descriptions of improvement in their children revealed that all of the parents in the experimental group and two-thirds of the parents in the placebo group believed that the child was "improved." The performance of the placebo group is of interest because it exactly matches Levitt's (1971) estimate of the proportion of disturbed children who will improve without treatment. The implication, of course, is that Levitt's estimates of spontaneous recovery are spuriously high.

The tendency of parents to overestimate treatment efficacy was also shown in two other studies. Patterson and Reid (1973) reported that observation and parent *daily* report data agreed in assigning 63% of a sample of treated families to an "improved" status. However, parents' *global* judgment data suggested 100% improvement. The authors would obviously like to accept the latter figure, but our clinical judgment suggests that we were really helping about two out of three families. Johnson and Christensen (1975) carried out a similar treatment study, using comparable criteria. Their observation data showed that 38% of the treated children showed significant improvement in their behavior, while parents' global judgments suggested that 93% had improved! A study by Schelle (1974) evaluated the validity of parental estimates of improvement on an extremely specific behavioral dimension: school attendance. He reported that for the group in which parental questionnaire data showed the greatest improvement, the actual school attendance data showed that the children were worse! While much more work must be done on this problem, it is the authors' opinion that pre- and post-test measures of parental global estimates of change in problem child behaviors will tend to overestimate treatment effects.

In retrospect, it seems likely that the *wrong questions* have been asked of parents. Global judgments have been elicited which require memory of events over long time spans. For example, some investigators have obtained information from mothers about child behaviors occuring over a twenty-four hour time period. In addition, parents have been required to use complex and/or poorly defined variables. A study by Douglas, Lawson, Cooper, and Cooper (1968) showed rather substantial correlations for parent and observers' data when the child behaviors were well defined. It would seem more reasonable to make more modest demands upon the parents and in the process perhaps obtain higher quality data. A laboratory study of three mother/child pairs by Peine (1970) showed promising results. Each mother/child pair participated in a series of five laboratory sessions in which the mother was asked to count well defined behavioral events as they occurred (e.g., such behaviors as "touch toys," "follows directions," "aggressive"). Many of the intra-subject correlations between observers and mothers were in the .80's and .90's. However, the mothers consistently underestimated the *level* of deviant behavior by as much as 600%! This finding is consistent with a study reported by Herbert (1970) in which low absolute agreement was found between observers and parents. It seems that under the best of conditions, parent data may provide an accurate estimate for the ordinal rankings of subjects but may underestimate actual mean level.

In our treatment research, *parent report* data are consistently collected at three different levels (Patterson, Reid, Jones, & Conger 1975). The levels vary in the specificity of the behaviors and the time intervals involved. First, parents are asked at termination to fill out rating scales which require global estimates of improvement such as those employed by Patterson and Reid (1973). In accord with our own findings and those of Johnson and Christensen (1975), it is expected that better than 90% of the parents will perceive some areas of improvement. At this level, parent global judgment is viewed as a necessary, but not sufficient, criterion for status as a success."[1]

Second, a method is used for obtaining more differentiated data from parents, which systematically samples centroid factors describing child personality. A significant change between pre- and post-ratings would be viewed as a necessary, but not sufficient, criterion for success status. The scales and scoring keys are to be found in Patterson, Reid, Jones, and Conger (1975).

Third, the Parent Daily Report (PDR) criterion has been developed to provide a more powerful criterion measure based upon parent data (Patterson, Cobb, and Ray, 1973). As part of the intake interview, the parents are asked whether each of the list of 31 "symptoms" are of sufficient concern to warrant changing. The list is published in Patterson, Reid, Jones, and Conger (1975). Parents are asked to collect data on the occurrence of these symptom behaviors during two weeks of baseline and at the end of treatment. These data are collected each day; the number of problems picked by each family usually ranges from three to nine. The parents indicate the occurrence or non-occurrence of each of those events during a given day. It is assumed that asking parents to make binary decisions (occur/non-occur), covering only the preceding eight to 10 hours, will minimize distortions in memory and judgment. The current practice is to express this score as mean frequency of symptoms per day.

The stability of this score over a two-week interval was analyzed by Patterson (1975). The (uncorrected) test-retest reliability was $R_{xy} = +.60$ ($df = 16$; $p < .01$). A study by Christensen (1976) obtained independent data from mothers and fathers for weekends. The correlations for the pairs ranged from $-.47$ to 1.00 with a mean of $+.51$. The mean frequency for PDR scores collected during baseline correlated $+.69$ ($df = 14$; $p < .01$) with a deviancy score (Total Deviant) derived from the observers' data collected during the same baseline period. The comparable correlation from the study by Fleischman (1976) was $+.46$ ($df = 21$; $p < .016$). The correlation from another study by Reid and Hinojosa (1977, in preparation) was $+.58$ ($df = 31$; $p < .001$). These findings suggest that the observers and the parents are in moderate agreement in ascribing a general level of deviancy to the problem child. Studies are currently underway to expand these pilot studies to more powerful analyses of the convergent and discriminant validities of the PDR score. In a treatment study, Patterson (1975) reported that 67% of a treated sample of children showed a reduction of at least 30% on the PDR score from baseline to treatment termination.

Waksman (1977) undertook a more definitive analysis of the relation between the two measures. Baseline data from 47 boys were subjected to an analysis of convergent and discriminant validity using the multi-trait multi-method procedure. There were six traits measured in common by the two methods: cry, yell, destructive, whine, noncomply, and negativism. The convergent correlation were significant for whine (.47); cry (.37); and for destructive (.33). The data showed moderate convergence for three of the six traits. However, only whine met the criteria for discriminant validity. The across method correlation for whine was greater than any of the within method correlations for whine with the other five traits. It was also greater than any of the across method correlations of whine with the other traits. The two methods vary not only in terms of the data source (parents vs observers) and format (informal vs systematic data) but also in terms of the time intervals involved.

1. The Walter and Gilmore (1973) and Wiltz and Patterson (1974) studies showed that four weeks of treatment were sufficient to produce significant changes in behavior. For this reason, *any* case receiving this much treatment was tallied as treated in evaluating success. This is in contrast to many of the traditional therapy studies which do not include data from these dropouts in evaluating treatment success rates. For example, two studies reviewed by Graziano and Fink (1973) showed uncounted dropouts of 40% and 60%!

The parents sample roughly sixteen hours a day and the observers only one. These differences make the findings even more surprising.

The PDR criteria may well turn out to be the first choice as an evaluation measure. Assuming that it survives further psychometric analyses, it has some definite advantages. First of all, it is a means for obtaining data describing low base rate events which are often foci for treatment but seldom seen by observers (e.g., fire-setting, truancy, stealing). Second, PDR is much less expensive to obtain than the observation data.

In current clinical practice, the PDR score constitutes one of our two major criteria for evaluating treatment. Its long range utility will be further defined by its correlation with police offense rates as the child moves through adolescence. In lieu of these data, which are now being collected, it might be noted that the PDR score at termination is the Oregon Social Learning Center's best predictor of status during follow-up. Using six months' follow-up data, the termination PDR score was in 83% agreement with the follow-up PDR score and in 58% agreement with the Total Deviant follow-up score. Again, success was arbitrarily defined as $\geq$ 30% decline from baseline levels.

The Family Interaction Coding System (FICS)

Early in the 1960's a social learning group (G.R. Patterson, D. Anderson, W. Bricker, M. Ebner, R. Littman, J. Reid, J. Straughan) had begun to form at the University of Oregon. Their concern with disturbed children led them into classrooms, homes, and institutions. A variety of techniques were tried as a means of collecting data. Narrative accounts were written in long-hand (Buehler, Patterson, & Furness, 1966) describing behavior and the environmental consequences supplied for it. To speed up this process, aggressive events were described on magnetic tape using the face-mask microphones and portable tape recorders developed by the Barker group (Schoggin, 1964). These tapes could then be transcribed and coded.

The general point of view which emerged emphasized the encoding of sequential events, i.e., *both* the child's behavior *and* the consequences provided by key social agents. This was further expanded to include continuous sequential accounts of the interaction of the child and family members. The first attempts used tapes dictated in the field setting (Patterson, McNeal, Hawkins, & Phelps, 1967). The cost of first transcribing and then coding these tapes was very high. The data analysis required endless tabulations. It was decided, therefore, to construct a code system that could be used in a field setting and readily punched and stored for computer analyses (Patterson & Reid, 1970; Reid, 1967).

Three years of preliminary studies were required for the development of a field observation code system. After six revisions, the data showed that the procedures provided reasonably complete descriptions of family interaction (Patterson, Ray, Shaw, & Cobb, 1969). The preliminary psychometric evaluations were promising (Patterson, Cobb, & Ray, 1973). It seemed that the field observation data collected in continuous sequential form was also effective in generating many hypotheses about aggressive behaviors occurring within families.

As an opening strategy, it was decided that learning could be maximized by focusing upon the assessment of a single type of problem, the severe Conduct Problem child. This meant giving up investments of clinical time already made to autistic and phobic children, and depressed adults as well. From the mid-1960's on, all of the time and energy in the reconstituted social learning group (G.R. Patterson, J. Reid, R. Ray, D. Shaw, J. Cobb, H. Hops and K. Skindrud) went into three different complex problems: (a) how to conceptualize the process of aggression; (b) how to treat families in which it occurred; and (c) how to measure it.

The first task faced by the developers of this observation system was to develop an item pool for observation. The "items" in this case were specific behaviors thought to be relevant to either the clinical or theoretical purposes of the assessment task. Clinical experience with socially aggressive children suggested some behaviors, but these behaviors had basically been gleaned from discussion with parents, teachers, and children, rather than directly observed in the child's natural environment. The investigators then ventured into the homes of families with young children in order to observe familial interaction and expand the behavioral code categories. Various methods of recording observed interaction were tried, ranging from long-hand note-taking following the observation session to the continuous reporting into a tape recorder mentioned earlier. The end result was a 29-category code system in which behavioral and environmental events were continuously coded. The sixth revision was described in the report by Patterson, Ray, Shaw, and Cobb (1969).

The code was designed to describe aggressive behaviors together with the antecedents and consequences which accompanied them. About half the code categories described such events; the other half included various prosocial behaviors. The revised code of twenty-nine categories used in the present study is listed in Table 1.

TABLE 1

Behavioral Code Definitions

AP	Approval	HU	Humiliate	PP	Physical Positive
AT	Attention	IG	Ignore	RC	Receive
CM	Command	IN	Indulgence	SS	Self-stimulation
CN	Command Negative	LA	Laugh	TA	Talk
CO	Compliance	NC	Non-compliance	TE	Tease
CR	Cry	NE	Negativism	TH	Touch
DI	Disapproval	NO	Normative	WH	Whine
DP	Dependency	NR	No Response	WK	Work
DS	Destructiveness	PL	Play	YE	Yell
HR	High Rate	PN	Physical Negative		

The family interaction was categorized into discrete units as it occurred. The observer alternately coded, in sequence, the behavior of the subject and then the person(s) with whom he interacted. Each event was described by code letters referring to the category(s) to which it was assigned together with the number(s) identifying the family member(s) with whom the target subject was interacting. If required, several subject numbers and code categories were used to describe an interaction. For example, a child could be crying and hitting at the same time.

The data were recorded continuously and provide a relatively complete, sequential account of the interaction of a target subject with all other family members. Every 30 seconds, the observer received an auditory signal from a device built into the clipboard (see schematic for building a timer in Appendix 2). At this point, the observer shifted to the next line of the protocol sheet. On the average, observers were able to record five interaction units (both members of a dyad) every 30 seconds.

Each night, the order in which family members were selected as target subjects was randomly determined. Each member served as target subject for five minutes and then the whole series was replicated. The observers keypunched the data shortly after returning from the field.

Observation sessions were semi-structured in that the families were instructed to remain within the home during the session and to keep the TV turned off. The following rules were instituted:

1. Everyone in the family must be present.
2. No guests.
3. The family is limited to two rooms.
4. The observers will wait only 10 minutes for all to be present in the two rooms.
5. Telephone: No calls out; *briefly* answer incoming calls.
6. No TV.
7. No talking to observers while they are coding.
8. Do not discuss *anything* with observers that relates to your problems or the procedures you are using to deal with them.

Structuring of this kind was deemed necessary. Our earlier attempts to use unstructured observation sessions resulted in parents and children wandering from room to room out of the observer's sight (and hence uncodable) or immersing themselves in a TV program, thus enabling them to escape interacting with other family members.

The coding system serves a two-fold purpose at the Oregon Social Learning Center. First, it provides data for evaluating treatment process and outcome (Arnold, Levine, & Patterson, 1975; Patterson, 1974a, 1975, 1976; Patterson, Cobb, & Ray, 1973; Patterson, Ray, & Shaw, 1968; Patterson & Reid, 1973; Reid & Hendriks, 1973; Walter & Gilmore, 1973; Wiltz & Patterson, 1974). It also provides data to support the development and validity of a theory of coercion and social aggression (Patterson, 1976; Patterson & Cobb, 1971, 1973; Patterson & Reid, 1970; Reid & Hendriks, 1973).

Behavior rates reported by the FICS provide one set of criterion variables for measuring the efficacy of intervention. Codes may be combined in any desired manner to produce cluster or composite categories such as "total deviant behavior" (all 14 coercive responses: DI, DP, DS, HU, HR, IG, NE, NC, PN, TE, WH, YE), hostility, (DI, NE, HU, IG, WH), social aggression (PN and TE), and total targeted behavior (summed behavior rates for behaviors targeted by family for change).

Other clusters of code categories can be used to describe changes in parental consequences for child behavior (Taplin & Reid, 1976), changes in the reactions of the problem child to parental punishment (Patterson, 1976), changes in the behavior of siblings following treatment (Arnold, Levine, & Patterson, 1975), or family "structure" prior to and following treatment (Patterson, 1976).

In the chapters which follow, many of the variables will be expressed as "rate per minute." Within the present context, it should be understood that the upper limit of the rate per minute would be approximately 10 responses per minute for any given subject. Because the coding system categorized the behavior of the target person every six seconds, what may have been "continuous" events become discrete occurrences, e.g., a child crying for 18 seconds would be coded as a sequence of three "Cry." For this reason, it is not possible to differentiate recurrence from duration.

Summary

Studies on the reliability and validity of parent global report data suggest that parents are unable to provide reliable global reports of their children's behavior. These global reports have been shown to be consistently biased in favor of improvement when, in fact, no change has occurred. The use of Parent Daily Report (PDR) data provides a more powerful criterion measure based upon parent data. Distortions in memory and judgement are minimized by asking parents to make binary decisions (occur/non-occur) on a list of specifically defined and easily counted behaviors which may have been observed during the preceeding eight to ten hours. The PDR criteria may well turn out to be a first choice as an evaluation procedure. Observational coding systems, with independent observers and well defined code categories, have been developed to provide reliable data on changes in family process. The Family Interaction Coding System (FICS) was designed to describe both aggressive and prosocial behavior. The data provide a relatively complete, sequential account of the interaction of a target subject with all other family members. The coding system serves a two-fold purpose at the Oregon Social Learning Center. It not only provides data for evaluating treatment process and outcome but also for the development of a theory of coercion and social aggression.

Chapter 3

The Observation System: Methodological Issues and Psychometric Properties

G. R. Patterson,
J. B. Reid, and S. L. Maerov

INTRODUCTION

As a data collection device, any given code system reflects the outcome of a number of arbitrary decisions, e.g., the content of what one observes, the number and size of the behavioral units, the use of frequency or duration measures, etc. However, once these decisions have been made, the resulting system is "just" an assessment device. Like any assessment device, an observational system should be evaluated in terms of the various psychometric properties subsumed under the traditional notions of reliability and validity. Modern systems of coding parent/child interactions reflect varying degrees of psychometric development (e.g., Bales, 1950; Bobbitt, Gourevitch, Miller, & Jensen, 1969; Caldwell, 1969; Moustakas, Sigel, & Schalock, 1956; Yarrow & Waxler, 1976). Contemporary reviewers of this new literature demonstrate increasing demands for sophistication in the analyses of these problems (Jones, Reid, & Patterson, 1975; Johnson & Bolstad, 1973; Lytton, 1971; Mash, 1976; Weick, 1968; Wiggins, 1973a).

Observer Agreement

Reliability is, of course, a basic requirement of any measurement system. Observer reliability in coding is defined as the degree to which observers code behaviors in accordance with some predefined criteria (e.g., a comparison of one observer's protocol (coding sheet) with that of another; a comparison of one observer's protocol to a precoded videotape of a family session). In our system, every third home observation session during baseline, and every fourth session thereafter is attended by two observers. The percentage agreement level is then calculated separately for each 30-second line on the protocol:

$$\frac{\text{number of frames of agreement}}{\text{number of frames of agreement} + \text{number of frames of disagreement}}$$

A frame is defined as a six-second time sample of behavior and is subdivided into two parts: the subject number* and antecedent behavior (part one) and the respondant's number* and consequation (part two). Agreement involves all four components. An instance of double-coding (two behaviors per subject or respondant) would be considered an additional interaction segment and would add to the denominator. Therefore, while one line on a rating sheet contains five six-second time samples, the total number of agreement points may exceed 10 points if either the subject or other family members emitted more than one

---
*See page 30 for an explanation of the family member numbering system.

behavioral response during any six-second time sample (or frame) on that line.

As Johnson and Bolstad (1973) point out, there are a large number of methods one *could* use in calculating observer agreement. Each has its own particular set of assets and liabilities. For some purposes, the technique outlined above might constitute an underestimate of agreement. For example, the stress upon correct notation of events *and* sequence could very well be irrelevant to tasks which require only an estimate of mean rate of occurrence. For these analyses, a more appropriate dependent variable could be the mean frequency of a given code category which is obtained from the *entire* protocol.

Calculating observer agreement on a line-by-line basis provides a general estimate of the quality of the data. Typically, these data on inter-observer reliability are obtained on a regular basis for project cases and posted on a bulletin board. It is expected that the values will *not* fall below a mean of 70% for a given observer pair on any given session. The average is around 75%. As pointed out by Cohen (1960) and others, the interpretation of this agreement score must take into account the level of chance agreement. His Kappa is a means of expressing agreement, taking into account chance level. This is a preferred method for analyzing observer agreement.

Numerous methods for appraising reliability measures exist, ranging from classical psychometric theory (e.g., Gulliksen, 1950) to generalizability theory (e.g., Cronbach, Glesser, Nanda, & Rajaratnam, 1972). Classical theories have dealt with parallel forms, internal consistency, and test/retest reliabilities as conceptually distinct indices of measurement precision with separate statistical procedures for assessing each. Generalizability theory encompasses all of these forms and provides a unified approach for assessing the influences on measurement precision due to similar instruments (parallel forms), temporal stability (test/retest) and different assessors (inter-observer agreement).

Within the generalizability analysis of the data collected using this observational system (Jones, Reid, & Patterson, 1975), three facets have been defined: (a) coders — two conditions (either regular or calibrating coder); (b) occasions or trials — number points at which data have been collected; and (c) subjects — each individual is a separate condition within the subjects facet (i.e., N subjects). The resultant facet design, in which a behavioral observation score is used as the dependent variable, is employed to obtain estimates of variance components by conventional ANOVA procedures. This analysis partitions the variance in the dependent variable among the facets of the experimental design. Variance components attributable to coders, occasions, subjects, and the interaction of these facets are then obtainable.

During a 10-weekday baseline or pre-treatment phase, each of 13 referred deviant boys and 17 normal control boys was observed by a regular and calibrating observer for five-minute time segments, on two different days of the 10-day baseline. The two samples of boys were analyzed separately, with each sample treated as a random sample of boys from populations of deviant and normal boys, respectively.

Five dependent variables were chosen for analysis, including Total Deviant (sum of frequencies for 14 deviant behaviors), Comply (CO), Non-comply (NC), Talk (TA), and a combination code with Play (PL) and Normative (NO) (Jones, Reid, & Patterson, 1975). Table 2 shows the variance component estimates, in percents, for the two samples of boys, for each of the five dependent variables. These estimates were obtained by standard analysis of variance procedures for this mixed model, with random conditions within occasions and subject facets, and fixed conditions within the coder facet.

Table 2

Variance Component Estimates (Percents) for Two Samples and Five Dependent Variables in a Three-Facet Design*

Behavioral score sample	PL + NO		Total Deviant		CO		TA		NC	
	Dev.	Nor.	Dev.	Nor.	Dev.	Nor.	Dev.	Nor.	Dev.	Nor
Facets										
Subjects (S)	43.72	27.16	79.44	0.00	.36	37.56	7.96	0.00	81.17	0.00
Coders (C)	.07	0.00	0.00	0.00	2.14	0.00	.23	.04	0.00	0.00
Occasions (O)	0.00	0.00	0.00	0.00	0.00	0.00	0.00	0.00	0.00	0.00
S X C	0.00	1.13	2.84	0.00	0.00	.38	0.00	0.00	5.25	0.00
S X O	52.02	70.02	12.05	81.37	74.98	53.36	85.87	95.10	10.36	54.18
C X O	0.00	.24	0.00	0.00	0.00	.26	0.00	0.00	0.00	0.00
Residual (SXCXO)	4.17	1.25	5.64	18.62	23.53	8.44	5.93	4.72	3.23	45.82

N.B. Percents do not total precisely 100.0 due to rounding in calculations
* Data from Jones, Reid, & Patterson (1975, p. 19)

The combined analysis of the PL + NO variable for Subjects and Subjects × Occasions facets combined accounted for approximately 96% of the variance in the deviant sample and about 97% in the normal sample. Since virtually no variance in either sample was accounted for by the Coders or Occasions facets, or their interaction, Jones, Reid, and Patterson (1975) concluded that inter-coder agreement and across occasions stability (over all subjects) were extremely high for this variable.

Analysis of Total Deviant scores for the deviant sample suggested that about 91% of the variance in the sample was attributable to Subject and Subject × Occasion facets. This was an expected finding as this composite category was designed to assess behavioral deviancy in samples of behaviorally deviant boys (Jones, Reid, & Patterson, 1975). The construct validity of the Total Deviant score is further supported by the results from the normal sample. Here, none of the variance was due to Subjects. Jones, Reid, and Patterson (1975) concluded that Total Deviant is not a suitable measure for normal samples, or at least not as suitable as for the deviant samples. It must be reiterated, however, that the FICS and Total Deviant categories were designed for use with deviant boys, not normal or non-deviant boys.

Of the remaining three scores shown in Table 2 none show important variance due to Coders or Occasions, further supporting the conclusion that over all subjects, agreement between observers and stability across time was substantial. Variance estimates for these other scores showed that most of the accountable variance was due to Subjects and/or the Subjects × Occasions interactions.

In brief, Jones, Reid, and Patterson (1975) concluded from this components of variance analysis:

> (a) variance due to Coders was trivial; hence, intercoder agreement was substantial; (b) variance due to Occasions was trivial; *hence, on the average,* subjects did not change homogeneously over time; (c) variance due to Subjects was large when the behavioral score was an appropriate or relevant measure for the sample; for example, Total Deviant accounted for substantial variance in the deviant sample, but not the normal sample; and (d) variance due to the Subjects × Occasions interaction was typically large for all behavioral scores, indicating that behavior varies substantially over time for individual subjects, and that the nature of this intra-individual variation is highly idiosyncratic. (pp. 67-68)

Results of generalizability analysis for generalizability coefficients resulted in the data noted in Table 3. Only one of the ten coefficients shown in this table was appreciably low, .54 for NC in the normal sample. Jones, Reid, and Patterson (1975) have suggested that either this measurement is not particularly relevant for samples of normal boys, or that the base rate of this behavior in normal samples is so low that the amount of sampling in the generalizability study was insufficient. The other behavioral scores in the two samples produced results which allow us to conclude that measurement of these subjects in different situations is not greatly influenced by measurement error, and hence, meets the essential reliability requirements of any clinical assessment procedure.

Biased Observers

Rosenthal (1966) has defined experimental bias as the extent to which experimenter effect or error is asymmetrically distributed about the "correct" or "true" value. In the present context, such distortions could take the form of a constant bias on the part of the observer. It could also occur as a function of the impact of observer presence on subjects. Only the former will be discussed in this section.

Conceivably some errors could arise because observers *intentionally* distort their data. While intentional errors in recording and computation have been reported in the literature (Azrin, Holtz, Ulrich, & Goldiamond, 1961; Rosenthal, 1966; Rosenthal & Fode, 1963; Rosenthal & Lawson, 1964), those reports have primarily related to student experimenters as data collectors for their instructors. The implications of observer error, whether intentional or not, must, however, be guarded against. The most likely mechanism would seem to be the situation in which the experimenter communicates his expectations to the observers and thus exerts a subtle influence upon the moment-by-moment coding decisions which they make. Although few studies have systematically assessed the effects of observer bias in the natural setting with human subjects, many researchers have taken measures to minimize its potential effects (cf. O'Conner, 1969; Thomas, Becker, &

TABLE 3

Generalizability Coefficients (Interclass Correlations)
for Each of Five Behavioral Scores in Two Samples
Over Both Subjects and Occasions*

Sample	Behavioral scores				
	Total deviant	PL + NO	CO	TA	NC
13 deviant boys	.96	.99	.77	.98	.94
17 normal boys	.81	.96	.98	.95	.54

*From Jones, Reid, and Patterson (1975)

Armstrong, 1968). A preliminary study by Kass and O'Leary (1970) showed that experiment expectations produced a small but significant effect on the data coded by one group of observers but not for another. However, additional studies from both the Stony Brook and the Oregon laboratories have not supported that finding.

Skindrud (1972) carried out one of the first well-controlled field studies testing for the effect of bias upon well-trained observers. These observers had had several years' field experience and regular (re)training sessions in applying an earlier version of the present code (Patterson, Ray, Shaw, & Cobb, 1969). Two different "calibrating observers" were employed over a period of several years. They had offices separated from the rest of the project and were kept uninformed of the status of the families being treated. The regular cadre, on the other hand, knew which families were in the clinical and which in the matched normal samples. They also knew for the clinical sample whether the family was in baseline, treatment, or follow-up. A comparison of the rates of deviant behavior obtained from the informed and uninformed observers showed no significant effects for either family status (clinical or normal) or for treatment status (baseline or termination). However, the small samples involved in this field study led to the decision to carry out a large-scale laboratory study.

In this study, Skindrud (1972) enrolled 28 observers (women from the local community) in an intensive three-week training program. They were trained to use the present code by viewing videotapes of parent/child interaction. The minimal level of accuracy required to participate in the remainder of the study was 70%. The trainees were then divided into three groups. One group was given a bias to expect the next series of 12 sessions to reflect a 30% increase in deviant child behavior. A second group was given a bias to expect a decrease. A third group was not instructed about experimenter expectations. There was no significant effect of bias upon the data coded by the observers. Even the trends were not in accord with the expectancies the experimenter had given to the groups. Thinking that perhaps the less reliable observers might reflect the bias, a separate post-hoc analyses was run for this sub-group. Again, there were no significant effects. When tested to determine their understanding and acceptance of the experimenter's expectancies, they showed they did understand.

A power analysis showed that groups of the size used in the second study were sufficient to detect a bias greater than 15%. Taken together, the studies suggested that if well trained observers are biased, the magnitude of the effect is not very large.

Kent, O'Leary, Diament, and Dietz (1974) replicated Skindrud's findings. Ten well trained observers were assigned to one of two groups. One group was told the next series of videotapes would show a child getting better and the other group that they would show a child getting worse. There was no significant effect of experimenter expectancies upon the data actually coded by the observers. In this analyses, they even sought for the effect by analyzing each code category separately. Experimenter expectancies were, however, dramatically reflected in the observers' global judgments. Ninety percent of the observers in the first group thought they detected an increase in the child's rate of deviant behavior. Seventy percent in the second group thought they detected a decrease.

In his 1972 investigation, Skindrud reported a pilot study in which he reinforced the observers for collecting data which were congruent with experimenter expectancies. Even with an N=6, he obtained changes in coded data which were of borderline significance. O'Leary, Kent, and Karpowitz (1975) carried out a study along the same lines and which closely paralleled field situations. Four observers viewed videotapes and were told to expect changes in two code categories. They were reinforced when their coded data were congruent with the experimenter's expectancies and punished when they did not. The changes in the data for the two target categories were in accord with the reinforcement contingencies while code categories not involved did not reflect these changes. While other, more carefully controlled studies should be carried out, the findings strongly emphasize the necessity for therapists *not* to provide observers with this type of feedback on their observations.

As the findings now stand, it does not seem that experimenter or therapist expectancies ipso facto bias the data collected by *well* trained observers. Expectancies *can* effect observers' global judgment about what is going on. Experimenters could perhaps bias their coded data by using reinforcement contingencies but this is not likely to happen in most well run field studies.

Observer Drift

Even if observer bias can be controlled, there is always the possibility that the quality of observation data may be compromised by a gradual change in the manner in which observers use the observational system. The first such possibility is that the observers may become less reliable after or between sessions during which their performance is monitored. Data in support of such a phenomenon have been reported frequently in the literature (e.g., DeMaster, Reid, & Twentyman, 1976; Reid, 1970; Taplin & Reid, 1973). A second possibility is that observers who work together will gradually drift in their use of code category definitions in such a way that their protocols agree with each other, *but differ from standard protocols*. Data to strongly suggest that this phenomenon can occur have been reported by DeMaster, Reid and Twentyman (1976), and by Romanczyk, Kent, Diament, and O'Leary (1971). A third way in which the quality of observation data may be underestimated by discontinuous reliability checks is due to the differential complexity of observational sessions. Reid, Skindrud, Taplin, and Jones (1973) have shown that the reliability of observational data is negatively correlated with the complexity of the behavior observed and that it is possible (perhaps unintentionally) for reliability assessments to be consistently carried out during sessions of low complexity. Thus, it is possible for reliability assessments to significantly *overestimate* the quality of observation data.

In order to guard against these problems, it is strongly advised that investigators: (1) carry out frequent reliability checks; (2) recalibrate observers regularly using standard video tapes; and (3) sample complex as well as simple interactions during reliability assessment in the field.

Observer Presence Effects

The heart of the observer presence problem lies in the fact that each of us has experienced being observed. We know full well that such an intrusion sets constraints upon some of our behaviors in some settings. The problem, of course, lies in the means by which we can delineate such affects empirically. An unpublished study by Paul (1963) suggests that mothers being observed in their homes also felt constrained. In that study, 10 mothers and their preschool children were observed over a 10-week period. The mothers reported feeling very much aware of the observers' presence throughout the study. However, mothers' ratings made during intervals when the observers were present and when absent showed no effects in the behavior of the child. The observation data supported none of the various hypotheses being tested relating to the impact of observer presence upon mother/child interaction.

One can conceptualize this problem in a variety of ways. However, the studies completed thus far seem to arrange themselves in terms of the following questions: (1) Do subjects being observed orient to the novel stimulus (observer presence)? (2) Does observation result in the generalized arousal of the subject, e.g., increase in social interaction rates? (3) Does observation elicit a set to suppress socially undesirable behaviors? Given extended exposure, the subjects may habituate to observer presence. This effect would be reflected in significant increases over sessions in rates of deviant behavior.

(1) Orienting to the observers. At one level, the question is simple. "Do subjects look at or talk to the observers?" As might be expected,

younger children are likely to be most overt and display high rates of such behavior. Adults are perhaps more circumspect. Observation data were collected in nursery schools by Connolly and Smith (1972). Their data suggest that observer presence did, in fact elicit high rates of orienting behavior, particularly during the first few sessions. Even though habituation effects were reported, the orienting behaviors did *not* fall to zero, even after eight sessions. Grimm, Parsons, and Bijou (1972) also noted high rates of such orienting behaviors in a classroom setting. They reported that the behaviors persisted over a six-month period in which the children were regularly observed. Candland, Dresdale, Leiphart, and Johnson (1972) noted that the behavior of non-human primates was affected, even after three years of being subjected to observation sessions. It seems safe to say that while families may eventually learn to talk less to observers and to stare at them less frequently, that they remain aware of their presence.

(2) Observer presence activates interactions. Much of what people do in a variety of different settings seems to be non-social in character, i.e., stare out the window, watch TV, work in the kitchen. One might assume that one effect of observer presence is to activate higher rates of whatever social behaviors the subject believes to be appropriate to that setting. The implicit assumption would be that observer presence would elicit a set to do less neutral behaviors and shift toward more task-oriented and/or more social behaviors.

Two studies carried out in classroom settings compared observers' presence to video camera presence. In a study by Mercatoris and Craighead (1973), observer presence significantly increased task-oriented interaction. A study by Surratt, Ulrich, and Hawkins (1969) showed significant increases in "time working" when observers were present. Similarly, a study by Moos (1968) compared the effects of a microphone-transmitter carried by psychiatric patients to being observed. When the psychiatric patients were in the day room setting, the effect of the observers was to elicit significantly higher rates of such socially appropriate behaviors as smile, talk with hands, looking at the speaker, and also play with object, arm and foot movements.

An observation study by Zergiob, Arnold and Forehand (1975) is most pertinent to this discussion. Twelve mother/child pairs were observed as they sat in a waiting room. On two successive visits, they were either informed or uninformed of the fact that they were being observed. Under the informed conditions, there was a significant increase in the amount of play interaction and in the mother's use of positive verbal comments and attempts to structure the interaction.

In all studies, the effect of observers' presence was significant. The effects seem to be an increase in some very *specific* task oriented or socially oriented behaviors. The shifts, however, would *not* be characterized a global attempt to look good. In fact, when attempts have been made to assess such behaviors (Mercatoris & Craighead, 1973), no significant changes in percent behaviors appropriate to that setting have been found. Nor were there decreases in deviant behaviors. It seems as if people select one or two setting appropriate behaviors and accelerate them when being observed.

In this context, one might again raise a question about the habituation of subjects to observer presence. In the Mercatoris and Craighead (1973) study, children were observed for 20 sessions. There was no evidence for a habituation hypothesis, e.g., significant changes in mean level over trials. Similarly, Patterson and Cobb (1973) and Johnson and Bolstad (1974) found no evidence for changes in mean level over sessions for family interaction. However, the later studies used only very limited samples of families and only six to 10 observation sessions. The designs lacked the power to identify any but the most gross changes.

Habituation effects can also be identified by using correlational analyses. For example, the subject's behavior observed in the first few sessions might inter-correlate but the earlier sessions might not correlate with later sessions. Such a correlational analysis of classroom behaviors by Masling and Stern (1969) did not support the variability hypothesis. Similarly, a home observation study by Paul (1963) failed to support it. A home observation study by Harris (1969) showed a trend for the data from observer present trials to correlate at low levels with data from observer absent trials. However, a family interaction study by White (1972) failed to replicate the trend.

In summary, the studies suggest that observers' presence has an effect which seems setting specific. The effects seem to be that of accelerating a small number of setting relevant behaviors. The effects do not seem to habituate over trials. It should be noted, however, that none of the studies testing the latter hypotheses used more than 20 sessions. This, in turn, sets severe limits upon any statements about habituation.

Manipulation of Sets to "Fake Good" and "Fake Bad"

There is a hint in the preceding section that subjects may adopt a set to "fake good" when they are aware of being observed. Although that effect was manifest in only a few setting specific responses, the tentative findings do suggest the need for a more direct test of the hypotheses. Such a test would involve the direct manipulation of the parents' set to make their child look "good" or "bad." Such studies have been designed and carried out by Johnson and Lobitz at the University of Oregon.

In the first study (Johnson & Lobitz, 1974), parents were instructed to make their young children look "bad or deviant" on three days of a six-day observation session, and to look "good" on alternate days. The observation data collected in the home showed that on "bad" days, there were significant increases in parental punishment and in parent commands. It was not clear from this study that the shifts in child behavior were significantly different from the child's normal levels of deviant behavior. In addition, it was not clear that the effects would be found among clinical samples of children from distressed families.

In a second study (Lobitz & Johnson, 1976), volunteer parents of younger children were used. One sample of 12 families had "problem children" as labeled by one or both parents. The other sample of 12 were presumably problem free. The parents were instructed on two consecutive days to make their child look good; then on two consecutive days to make him look bad and on two consecutive days he was to look normal. Families were randomly assigned to one of the six possible orderings of these conditions. The results showed that the parents in both samples produced significant increases in deviant child behaviors when comparing "look normal" to "look bad" conditions. Ten of 12 deviant families and nine of 12 non-problem families seemed effective in producing this shift. These shifts were accompanied by significant increases in parental commands and punishment and a significant decrease in their positive consequences. The data from the combined sample showed no significant shift in child behavior from normal to the good conditions. Seven of 12 non-problem families were effective in producing this shift whereas only four of 12 in the problem sample were successful. Questionnaires given the parents showed that they generally perceived themselves more effective in accelerating good behavior than in accelerating bad behavior! Again, parent perceptions of behavior change were not in accord with observations of the same behavior events.

These findings suggest then that it is quite possible that some estimates of baseline data for problem families *could* be spuriously inflated. The Lobitz and Johnson (1976) data showed a 105% increase over normal conditions in the rate of deviant child behaviors when parents of problem children were instructed to make their children look bad. It is conceivable, then, that at termination they reduce their rates of commands and punishment and thus "allow" the child to reduce his rate to a significant degree. While this is plausible, data analyzed by Taplin (1974) showed that after treatment the significant reductions in deviant child behaviors were accompanied by non-significant *increases* in the proportion of problem behaviors punished. No data were analyzed for pre- and post-treatment comparisons of parent command rates. The analyses by Patterson (1975) provided support for the notion that the changes in deviant child behavior were produced by an increase in the *impact* of parental punishment in suppressing ongoing coercive child behavior.

The studies by Johnson and Lobitz emphasize the necessity for current family intervention studies to show process changes, e.g., in parenting behavior, as well as to demonstrate reductions in deviant child behaviors. They also suggest that family interaction data may reflect parental sets to make their families look bad but probably reflect the set to look good to only a limited degree. There is, of course, the alternative hypothesis that current data already reflect the efforts of the parents to make their child look good and heightened sets could therefore achieve but little. However, pending further expansion of research in this area, it seems reasonable to assume that both parents and children find it difficult to "fake good" over extended periods of time. It seems possible that habitual modes of interacting provide powerful constraints for familial interaction patterns. Presumably, these constraints are more effective in controlling behavior than is a set to look good. Perhaps the immediate shift in positive behaviors on the part of the child are not enough to maintain parental positive behaviors. It is also possible that the child fails to reciprocate, e.g., increase reinforcement contingent upon the sudden increase in parent positive behaviors. In either instance, the net effect would be a short term, minimal increase in parent positive behaviors. Increases in parental aversive behavior would, on the other hand, increase the probability that children would respond in kind (Kopfstein, 1972; Patterson & Cobb, 1971; Rausch, 1965).

Unobtrusive Measures and Deception Studies

One would hope to have some unobtrusive measure which would provide an absolute base for comparing the effect of observers being present to their not being present. While there are no studies which successfully bring this about, several investigators have made innovative approximations.

Purcell and Brady (1966) equipped 13 boys in a residential treatment center with radio transmitting devices. Raters coded the transcripts of their interactions according to a set of personality trait dimensions. Another set of data was collected by observers using Barker's technique for obtaining specimen records. The mean correlation between the two modes of data collection was .79. Parents rated the boys before and during the study. There was no significant change in their behavior as a function of the observers and radio transmitter. This latter finding was in accord with the data from mothers' ratings of preschool child behaviors emitted prior to and again during the observation session (Paul, 1963).

Bernal, Gibson, Williams and Pesses (1971) experimented with the placement of an audio tape recorder in the home of a mother and her three children. Over a six-week period, the observer was present for one session per week; recordings were made for seven-minute intervals four times each day throughout the period. Family members were aware of when it was that the two sets of data were being collected. The correlation over days between the two modes of data collection was +.89 ($p < .02$) for the response "mother command." It was interesting to note that the rates were lower for the audio tape than for data from observers in the home. Johnson and Bolstad (1974) replicated and extended this basic design to include 12 families of younger children (ages 4–8). One hour prior to dinner time, an audio recorder was turned on; all family members were aware of the arrangement. Over the six-day period, observers were present at that same time on alternate days. The data from the audio tapes showed no significant effect for the observers' presence or absence on the occurrence of deviant child behaviors. Correlational analyses also showed observer presence or absence did not effect children's or parents' ordinal rankings for aversive behaviors. The Mercatoris and Craighead (1973) classroom study followed a similar and more extended ABAB design using a video camera instead of a tape recorder. The analyses showed no difference for observers' presence or absence on percent of appropriate or percent of inappropriate behaviors.

All of these studies are consistent in concluding that observer presence does not produce significant changes in behavior from those obtained by audio or video recordings. These conclusions are reached whether one searches for alterations in ordinal rankings or changes in mean level. This is not to say, of course, that the mechanical recordings do not themselves represent distortions from normal interaction levels.

Two deception studies have been carried out which attempt to get at the problem of estimating absolute level. Harris (1969) trained 15 mothers as observers to 80% agreement. They were then randomly assigned to one of three groups. For the outside observer (OO) group, mothers from other families served as observers who collected data for six sessions. For the mother-observer (MO) group, the mothers collected data for three sessions in their own homes. During the last three sessions, an outside observer collected the data. When the mother collected the data, the families were told that the mother who was wearing dark glasses was participating in a psychology experiment to determine the impact of social interaction on encoding perceptual symbols. In the third group, the mothers (MM) coded the entire six sessions for their own families. In all three groups, the subjects were fathers interacting with their children. The mean proportion of social interaction for the groups in the various conditions is recorded in Table 4.

TABLE 4

Mean Rates of Social Interaction

Groups	Sessions 1–3	Sessions 4–6
OO	.52	.89
MM	.86	.87
MO	.87	.72

It was predicted that the impact of the outside observer would be to increase socially desirable behaviors, i.e., social interaction. However, a 3×3 ANOVA for repeated measures showed that none of the main effects nor interaction terms were significant. In fact, even the trends for two of the three relevant comparisons were in the opposite direction from that predicted. A comparable analysis for rates of total deviant child behavior also produced non-significant results.

In retrospect, it seems possible that the mother observers might have dropped markedly in their reliability following their training program. In that Harris did not carry out any reliability checks during her experiment, the lack of findings could have been due to the unreliability of the data. Second, there were enormous differences among families in their rates of deviant behavior and in the rates of social interaction. A study using such a small N might not have the power necessary to test for subtle effects. With these qualifications in mind, White (1972) used trained professional observers, a larger N (25), and shifted the setting from the laboratory to the home. He also used an $A_1 B_1 A_2 B_2$ repeated measures design involving four, 30-minute sessions. During the observer absent periods, A_1 and A_2, the mothers and their children were told they were "waiting" for the observers. During B_1 and B_2, an observer appeared and coded their interactions while sitting in the same room with them. Actually the family was observed by concealed observers who coded their interactions in all four settings. The ANOVA for repeated measures showed no significant effects for either the families' rates of social interaction or the total deviancy rates. The findings essentially replicated the results reported by Harris (1969).

Perhaps the best conclusion from these deception studies is that if an observer presence effect exists, it is of small magnitude. It is most likely reflected in the relative absence of some of the more pathological behaviors found in family interactions. For example, while we see some hitting behaviors, we have observed only a few beatings. Clinically, we have reason to believe the latter occurs at a higher rate than shown in our data. The fact that such low base rate behaviors may not occur when the observer is present is a problem of some moment. It is, however, our growing impression that habitual patterns of family interaction set their own powerful constraints. If the typical mode is that of coercive interchanges, then they will persist when the observers are present with only those paths filtered out which lead to escalating high amplitude interchanges. In the more disturbed families, even these paths can not be filtered and the observer can readily see parents assaulting children and children physically attacking each other.

Summary

In retrospect, it seems that for the study of family coercive interchanges, the variables of greatest concern turn out to be relatively free of "noise." Certainly the problem of observer presence does exist. Undoubtedly it contributes to some distortion in the data. But studies to date suggest that the problem is *not* of the magnitude anticipated by us when we began our work 10 years ago. At that time, the problem of observer bias also loomed large on the horizon. The studies carried out to date suggest that for well trained observers, it is *not* a major problem. The problem of the drop in reliability when observers are not monitored is a major source of noise in the data. With careful retraining, recalibrating, and continued assessment, the level of such noise can be controlled.

Chapter 4

Coding of Family Interactions

S. L. Maerov, B. Brummett,
G. R. Patterson and J. B. Reid

The behavioral coding system described in this chapter is designed to provide a sequential account of social interaction among family members. The code is meant to be simple to understand and use so that little inference is required on the part of the observer to determine the appropriate code for a behavior.

To facilitate learning to code family interactions, this chapter is divided into four sections. The first section will provide a definition for each behavioral category; the second will describe the proper use of the code system; the third will discuss data collection procedures; and the fourth will provide a narrative account of a typical family situation, accompanied by a completed code sheet, accurately recording the behaviors of the family members. Chapter 5 provides additional observer training procedures.

Code Categories

It is impossible to code every behavior emitted. Often a person will emit three or four behaviors simultaneously. In order to limit the number of behaviors attributable to one individual to two per three-second sequence, behaviors are designated as either First-Order Behaviors or Second-Order Behaviors on the basis of their presumed relevance for evaluating treatment or their relation to a theory of social learning. Observers will utilize Second-Order code categories *only* when they are unable to describe the on-going behavioral interaction with First-Order codes. Second-Order codes cover behaviors deemed less significant in the analysis of family interaction from a diagnostic, treatment, and theoretical point of view.

Behavioral Code Definitions

The 29 behavior codes listed in alphabetical order are:

AP	Approval	NE	Negativism
AT	Attention	NO	Normative
CM	Command	NR	No Response
CN	Command Negative	PL	Play
		PN	Physical Negative
CO	Compliance		
CR	Cry	PP	Physical Positive
DI	Disapproval		
DP	Dependency	RC	Receive
DS	Destructiveness	SS	Self-stimulation
HR	High Rate	TA	Talk
HU	Humiliate	TE	Tease
IG	Ignore	TH	Touch
IN	Indulgence	WH	Whine
LA	Laugh	WK	Work
NC	Non-compliance	YE	Yell

To aid the observer in learning the codes, the behavior codes have been divided into categories: verbal, non-verbal, or a combination of the two. Behaviors are listed alphabetically within each sub-area. An alphabetical index of the code definitions is provided at the end of the chapter.

First-Order Code Categories

First-Order Verbal Behaviors
(CM, CN, CR, HU, LA, NE, WH, YE)

CM (COMMAND): This category is used when a direct, reasonable, and clearly stated request or command is made to another person. The verbal statement must clearly specify the behavior which is expected from the person to whom the command is directed. The code system requires that either compliance or noncompliance be coded within 12 seconds. If the command requires compliance in the future, code TA.

Examples of CM:
1. "Johnny, it's time to pick up your toys."
2. "Bring me the newspaper from the table."
3. "June, please set the table."

Examples of Non-CM:
1. At the dinner table, Mother requests, "Please pass the salt." Code TA. In play or meal settings where *routine statements* of direction or requests tend to be made at a high rate (i.e., "Pass the salt" at the dinner table; "roll the dice" when playing parcheezi), these requests should be coded TA, PL, or other appropriate codes. Do not code them as CM. This coding decision is an idiosyncracy of our code. We are concerned with the relationship between CM and CO, but are not interested in an inflated CM:CO ratio which would occur when coding natural response patterns characteristic of common situations.
2. "Next week, Pam, you are to wash the car." Code TA. This is an example of a future command (i.e., one in which compliance will occur after the end of the observation session). Future commands are coded TA or other appropriate codes depending upon the characteristics of the statement and the situation at hand.
3. "Jimmy, can't you help?" Code DI. There does not appear to be an explanation of Jimmy helping as the statement was *not* made as a direct request, but rather as a question presented in a critical tone of voice. This statement represents an indirect manner of questioning help rather than *directly* requesting action. The appropriate code for this situation would be DI.

CN (COMMAND NEGATIVE): A negative command differs from the *reasonable* command in the manner in which it is delivered. This kind of command must be characterized by *at least one* of the following: (1) immediate compliance is demanded; (2) aversive consequences are *implicitly* or actually threatened if compliance is not immediate; (3) sarcasm or humiliation is directed toward the receiver. Implicit use of aversive consequences is indicated by the tone of voice as well as the statement.

Examples of CN:
1. "Stop that *right* now!"
2. "You are *going to get it* if you don't stop teasing your sister."
3. "You *get off* my coloring book, *you dummy!*"

Examples of Non-CN:
1. "Clean off the counter. I don't like it when you leave it sticky." Code CM/DI. This is not coded CN because it is a clear, reasonable request and a clearly stated disapproval of the behavior of the person, reasonably delivered.
2. Situation: Mother has commanded John to set the table; he has said "yes" but continues to play. Several frames later she says in a disapproving, disgusted fashion, "JOHNNIE!" Code this DI rather than CN because mother is implying that the child should stop his inappropriate behavior and attend to the task at hand. She is not implying aversive consequences or using humiliation or sarcasm in addressing the child.
3. "Why don't you shape up!" (said in an

impatient manner). Code DI because the statement is more a comment on the quality or quantity of another's behavior than a direct request for behavioral change.

CR (CRY): Use this category whenever a person sobs or cries tears. Actual tears do not have to be present.

HU (HUMILIATE): This category is used when a person makes fun of, shames, or embarrasses another person. *The tone of voice* (in terms of nastiness or derisiveness), as well as the language used, is of prime importance in meeting the criteria for coding HU. Derisive or inappropriate laughter can also be humiliating. Playful verbal statements or nicknames are not humiliations. Some people call each other "stupid" more in terms of endearment than in humiliation.

Examples of HU:

1. "You dumb old grouch!" (said in a derogatory fashion).
2. "How did you get 90 on your test. You must have cheated."
3. "Don't you even know how to color right?" (said in a contemptuous way).

Examples of Non-HU:

1. The difference between HU and playful banter is a function of delivery, inflection, and facial expression. Often the words are the same but done in a mild and/or endearing way, as in replying to a remark with "You turkey face," with a laugh. Comments of endearment said in a playful fashion are coded TA.

LA (LAUGH): Whenever a person laughs aloud pleasantly and in an agreeable manner, code LA. Simultaneous talking and laughing, code only LA.

Examples of LA:

1. A person laughs at a joke.
2. Chuckles at item in a newspaper.
3. Amused giggling when listening to conversation of others.

Examples of Non-LA:

1. Mother laughs at a child who just reported failing an exam. Code HU. Laughing as a form of "put down" is coded HU.

NE (NEGATIVISM): This category is used only when a person makes a statement in which the verbal message is neutral, but which is delivered in a tone of voice that conveys an *attitude* of "don't bug me," or "don't bother me." Also included are defeatist, "I-give-up" statements (see 2 below). This code is never to be used if the *verbal* meaning of the statement is interpreted as disapproving (DI) or humiliating (HU).

Examples of NE:

1. Code pouting NE if it implies "don't bug me."
2. "I give up. No matter what I do, I can't do it. I can try 100 times, but I can't get it. You can show me all you want, but I can't."
3. "What's that to me? Who cares?"

Examples of Non-NE:

1. Mother CMs your subject; then she turns away. The subject makes a face at mother behind her back. Code DI because the subject is disapproving of mother's behavior in a non-verbal manner.
2. Father talks in a derogatory manner about his boss. He becomes sarcastic and negative. Code TA because NE is not directed to a family member.

WH (WHINE): When a person uses a slurring, nasal, or high-pitched voice, use this category. The content of the statement can be of an approving, disapproving, or neutral quality; the main element is the voice quality.

YE (YELL): This category is to be used whenever a person shouts, yells, or talks loudly. The sound must be *intense enough* that it is unpleasant or potentially aversive if carried on for a sufficient length of time.

First-Order Non-Verbal Behaviors (DS, HR, PN, PP)

DS (DESTRUCTIVENESS): This category applies to behavior in which a person *destroys, damages, or attempts to damage anything* other than a person; attacks on *persons* are coded PN.

The damage need not actually occur, but the *potential* for damage must exist, e.g., grabbing another's breakable materials. The value of the object is of no consideration, nor is the actual amount of damage done.

Examples of DS:

1. Any playing or climbing on furniture not intended for such activity is coded DS unless such activity was requested by a parent.
2. Hitting or lifting a dog by his collar and choking him is DS.
3. A person defiantly threatens to destroy or actually begins to destroy a toy or another object.

Note: Accidental breakage must still be coded DS.

Examples of Non-DS:

1. A child attacks his brother, grabbing his shirt and shoving him. Code PN. Damage in this case is directed at a person rather than at an object.

HR (HIGH RATE): This code is used for any very physically active, repetitive behavior not covered by other categories that, if carried on for a sufficient period of time, would become aversive. If the behavior can be coded by other categories, i.e., YE, PN, DS, then HR is not to be used. HR may be intermittently coded with other specific deviant behaviors. The prime goal in coding HR is to represent symbolically the observed behavior as occurring excessively as measured by its frequency and/or intensity. High rate behavior is the culmination of a series of behaviors which have accelerated until they have reached an intolerable level as judged by the observer.

Examples of HR:

1. Running back and forth repeatedly in the living room.
2. Child is seen yelling and flailing his body in a temper tantrum (code HR rather than YE because of the intensity of the child's behavior and the physical component to his activity).
3. Roughhousing. (Defined as extremely active physical play in close inappropriate confines.)

PN (PHYSICAL NEGATIVE): Use whenever a subject physically attacks or attempts to attack another person. The attack must be of sufficient intensity to *potentially inflict* pain, i.e., biting, kicking, slapping, hitting, spanking, or taking an object roughly from another person. The circumstances surrounding the act need not concern the observer, only the potential of inflicting pain.

Examples of PN:

1. Children playing and part of the play involves wrestling. If, during the wrestling, one child hits the other child or pins him down to the point where pain could result.
2. A child abruptly yanks away a toy from a sibling.
3. Mother grabs a child's arm and shoves the child.

Examples of Non-PN:

1. Child shadow-boxes with father. It begins as play, then actual physical contact begins. Code PL until blows become more intense. Observer uses his/her discretion to decide when to begin coding PN. (Play becoming aversive due to the intensity of hits would be coded PN.)

PP (PHYSICAL POSITIVE): This code is used when a person caresses or communicates with touch to another person in a friendly or affectionate manner.

Examples of PP:

1. A hug, a pat, a kiss.
2. An arm around shoulders, holding hands, ruffling hair, stroking, or caress.
3. Picking up a crying baby and comforting it is PP.

Examples of Non-PP:

1. An accidental brushing against another person. In other words, *unintentional* neutral body contact. Code TH or other appropriate code reflecting the behavior being emitted.

First-Order Verbal or Non-Verbal Behaviors (AP, CO, DI, DP, IG, IN, NC, PL, TE, WK)

AP (APPROVAL): Approval is a clear indication of positive interest or involvement. It is more reinforcing than Attend (AT). AT is neutral or non-directive response whereas AP has reinforcing characteristics. Approval can be gestural or verbal in nature and need not be elaborate or lengthy, but should be used to indicate even the smallest positive gesture. Approval is directed at behavior, appearance, or personal characteristics of an individual. It *does not* include the granting of permission to carry out an activity. That is coded TA.

Examples of AP:
1. Smiles, head nods.
2. Phrases such as "that's a good boy," "thank you," and "that's right."
3. Compliments such as "that dress looks nice on you."

Examples of Non-AP:
1. Mother grants a child's request, saying, "That's all right." Code TA because mother is not approving of anything the child did.
2. A child is working quietly on school work. Father goes by and pats her on the shoulder. Code PP because father is giving a physical positive rather than approving of her work.

CO (COMPLIANCE): Use this category when a person does what is asked or indicates verbally or behaviorally that he will. Compliance need not follow the CM, CN, or DP immediately; other behavioral sequences can intervene. However, the indication of compliance *must occur within 12 seconds of a behavior coded as CM or CN*. Delay of compliance beyond 12 seconds is NC. Commands which require compliance *after a period of 12 seconds* would not be coded CM or CN, nor would the agreement to comply be coded CO. Both the request and response indicating compliance would be coded TA or possibly DI. These are examples of what might be called future commands (see Example 2 of Non-CO).

Examples of CO:
1. Suzie gets up within 12 seconds and gets the paper when requested to do so.
2. Johnny says, "Okay, Mom, I'll do it" within 12 seconds after being asked to clear the table.
3. No more PNs occur within 12 seconds of a CN to stop hitting.

Examples of Non-CO:
1. When chains of commands occur, i.e., "pick up the dishes, scrape the scraps into one dish, collect silverware on the end of the table," and so on, compliance is clearly impossible. It is required that each CM and CN be consequated by either NC or CO before another command is coded. Therefore, NC must be used when there is no time allowed to comply.
2. Father: "John, please take out the garbage after dinner." John: "Okay, Dad." Code TA. Father's request of John is such that compliance cannot be coded within 12 seconds. As a result, the request must be coded TA. John's verbal response must also be coded TA because actual compliance will not be observed within the time allotted for the observation.

DI (DISAPPROVAL): Use this category whenever a person gives a verbal or gestural criticism of another person's behavior or characteristics. In verbal statements, it is essential that the content of the statement *explicitly* states criticism or disapproval of the subject's behaviors or attributes, looks, clothes, possessions, etc. DI can be coded simultaneously with CM but never with CN, as CN always implies disapproval. Code DI only when verbal disapproval (i.e., "I do not like you doing that") or gestural disapproval is implied by facial expression, vigor of the gesture, or the critical tone of voice. In addition, a DI can only be coded if either the subject or the person interacting with the subject directs the DI at the other member of the dyad. Disapproval of a third person would be coded TA.

Examples of DI:
1. Shaking the head or finger are examples of gestural disapproval.
2. "I do not like that dress," "You didn't pick up your clothes again this morning," "You're eating too fast," are examples of verbal disapproval.
3. A parent scowls or glares in anger at a child when milk is spilled. (The parent's look of disgust at the inappropriate behavior qualifies this example for coding as DI.)

Examples of Non-DI:
1. One person is critical of another person not present, i.e., school mate, fellow worker, boss, etc. The disapproval is not directed to a family member, but about another person. Code TA.
2. Child is asked a factual question and gets it wrong. Parent says, "No, that's not it." (This is an example of correcting a response rather than disapproving of a behavior.) Code TA.
3. Mother disciplines her son; he in turn mimicks the way she scolded him. Code HU because he is ridiculing her rather than disapproving of her.

DP (DEPENDENCY): Behavior is coded DP when a person is requesting assistance in doing a task that he is obviously capable of doing himself. Everyday requests should not be coded DP — for example, requests made at dinner would be coded TA unless the statement falls under the rules for coding CM. To code a behavior DP, it must meet two criteria: the person is capable of doing the act himself, and it is an imposition on the other person to fulfill the request.

Examples of DP:
1. A child, age 10, asks his mother to tie his shoes.
2. Mother is asked by a three- to four-year old to feed him.
3. Mother is cooking and is requested by an eight-year-old to help him find a missing part of a game.

Examples of Non-DP:
1. Father is getting the newspaper. The subject's schoolbook lies beside it. The subject requests that father hand the book to him. Code subject CM rather than DP as it was a reasonable request to make because his father was close to the book. DP would be coded if the child's request would have appeared to cause the father an inconvenience in responding.

IG (IGNORE): Ignore is an intentional and deliberate non-response to an initiated behavior. There is no doubt that the subject has heard but has chosen not to respond.

Examples of IG:
1. A child says directly to father, "Dad, I was chosen for math monitor today." Father has heard but does not look at her, then speaks to another member of the family about another matter.
2. Child touches mother and asks a question. Mother turns away or walks away.
3. Mother and father are talking. Father begins to read the newspaper. He does not in any way respond to her continued conversation.

Examples of Non-IG:
1. Father is absorbed in a magazine. The target child being coded speaks to him from across the room. Father continues reading. Code father's response as NR rather than IG because there was no clear indication father heard the child and attempted to avoid a recognition response.

2. A subject speaks to three or more persons in a non-directed way, "Where is the newspaper?" No one responds. Code subject TA, response 9NR (number refers to family member identification system; see page 30) because the behavior is not directed to any one person.

IN (INDULGENCE): Behavior is coded IN when, *without being asked*, a person stops what he is doing in order to do some behavior for another person which that person is fully capable of doing for himself. Common kindness, i.e., pouring a cup of coffee for another while also pouring one's own, handing a nearby dictionary to someone who has asked how to spell a word, are not to be coded IN. The helping person *must stop his own ongoing chain of behavior* and perform an *unnecessary* service for a capable person. Generally, the consequence of IN is RC. Care must be taken to distinguish this category from DP and WK.

Examples of IN:

1. The family members are eating; only father is drinking coffee. Mother notices that his cup is empty, stops feeding the baby, gets up and refills his cup.
2. An older sibling takes off a seven-year-old child's coat, and washes the child's hands before dinner.
3. Father cuts meat for a child old enough to do it for himself.
4. Mother does her son's arithmetic problems for him rather than helping him.

Examples of Non-IN:

1. Mother feeds an infant in a high chair. Code WK because the child is too young to feed himself.
2. Father asks mother to get up and bring him another slice of bread while she is feeding the baby. Code DP because father is requesting that mother stop what she is doing in order to do something for him which he is capable of doing for himself.

NC (NON-COMPLIANCE): This code is used when a person does not do what is requested of him in response to a CM, CN or DP within 12 seconds of the request being made. Non-compliance can be verbal or non-verbal in nature. Care must be taken to distinguish DI from NC.

Examples of NC:

1. Mother asks son to set the table. He says, "I don't want to."
2. Father, in a calm voice, says, "Stop that arguing." The children continue to bicker.
3. A child keeps his brother's toy when requested to return it.

Examples of Non-NC:

1. Mother tells daughter to do dishes. Daughter complains that she is always being asked to work. Daughter goes to the sink and begins to do the dishes. Code 3CM 4DI/CO (i.e., mother #3 commands, daughter #4 disapproves, but complies within 12 seconds of when command was made).
2. A person complies with the CM, CN, or DP *within* 12 seconds. Code CO because he complied.

PL (PLAY): This category is used when a person is amusing himself, either alone or with other people. Play need not be restricted to games in which clear rules are defined, i.e., monopoly, scrabble, or card games, but is applicable to many activities such as amusing oneself alone, with a pet, or playing with toys. Play can be verbal or non-verbal.

Examples of PL:

1. Playing with a pet may or may not involve verbalization.
2. Card games and the considerable conversation about the game are coded PL.
3. Coloring or drawing pictures.

Examples of Non-PL:

1. A child aimlessly manipulates a non-toy, i.e., a matchbook or string. Code NO, not PL, because the behavior appears to be aimless repetition or fiddling rather than a form of play behavior with any apparent direction or intent.

2. A child lies on the floor in a daydream manner and traces the patterns on the rug. Code NO because the child does not appear to be playing.

TE (TEASE): Teasing is defined as the act of annoying, pestering, mocking, or making fun of another person. Teasing behavior is directed in such a manner that the other person is likely to show displeasure and disapproval. This behavior is potentially provocative and disruptive to the other person.

Examples of TE:
1. A child is trying to do homework and another child keeps tickling him in the ribs or turns the pages of the book that the child is using for studying.
2. In a sing-song voice one child says to another, "You got in trouble and I didn't."
3. Taking a sibling's pawn or cards in a game or rearranging the game order. Peeking at another's hand during cards.

Examples of Non-TE:
1. The subject is playing alone and humming a tune repetitiously. It annoys a sibling who requests him to stop. The subject stops. (The humming is not a tease because the behavior cannot be inferred to be deliberate.) Code PL.
2. People calling each other names in an obviously endearing fashion, i.e., the names don't provoke aversive responses from their recipients, and are coded TA rather than TE or HU.

WK (WORK): Work is a behavior necessary to maintain the smooth functioning of a household; it is necessary for a child to perform work in order to learn behaviors that will help him to assume an adult role. A definite service performed for another person is also coded as WK.

Examples of WK:
1. Cooking, serving, kitchen-related activity.
2. School-related activities, hobbies, music practice.
3. Repairing a toy, combing a sibling's hair, and doing chores.

Examples of Non-WK:
1. Reading can be coded in two contexts. Reading a novel for a school report is coded WK. However, it must be clear that this is an assignment. The observer cannot assume reading is school work unless a clear communication is given of this fact. If in doubt, code NO.
2. On impulse, the subject sits down to the piano and plays a tune. Code PL rather than WK because playing was done for own amusement rather than specifically to have a particular skill.

Second-Order Code Categories

Categories in this section are used ONLY when it is inappropriate to use First-Order codes.

Second-Order Verbal Behaviors (TA)

TA (TALK): This code covers the exchange of conversation between family members. It is used if *none* of the other verbal codes are applicable. Do not use TA in cases where Talk is part of the ongoing activity required in PL or WK. Thus, in a game where one person says, "It's your turn," that is not coded TA, but simply as PL. Likewise, in a work situation when one member of a dishwashing team says, "Here are some more dishes," the proper code is WK and not TA.

Examples of TA:
1. Two siblings having an ongoing conversation about the day's activities.
2. Mother and father exchanging small talk.
3. General family conversation at the dinner table.
4. A child talks to mother about school activity. She says, "uh-huh" or "hmmm." Code this as TA.
5. Family member reads aloud to a child.

Second-Order Non-Verbal Behaviors (AT, NO, NR, RC, TH,)

AT (ATTENTION): This category is to be used when one person listens to or looks at another person. Attending behavior may either be initiated by a person or may be in response to another person's behavior. Sometimes, when listening is used as a reason for coding AT, it may be difficult to tell if the person is, in fact, listening. In general, unless eye contact or some form of verbal recognition is offered by persons supposedly listening to another person, the behavior of the respondent would be coded NR. Some form of non-verbal recognition is necessary before a person's behavior would be coded AT. A brief glance should not be coded AT when it is an initiation.

Examples of AT:

1. Father speaks to mother. She looks at him while he explains his point.
2. The subject listens to and watches mother and father talking to each other. This is an example of AT as an initiated behavior.
3. One child is playing alone; other persons in the room are watching him.

Examples of Non-AT:

1. A family member nods her head, smiles broadly as another member talks. Code this behavior AP because a smile is to be considered a form of approval.
2. Hmmm or uh-huh is coded TA because it is a verbal response whereas AT is a non-verbal behavior in this code.

NO (NORMATIVE): The normative code is used for routine behavior when no other code is applicable.

Examples of NO:

1. The family is eating dinner.
2. Someone is reading for pleasure.
3. Someone is walking from one room to another or looking out a window.

NR (NO RESPONSE): Use this code when a behavior does not require a response, or when a behavior is directed at another person but the person to whom the behavior is directed fails to perceive the behavior.

Examples of NR:

1. Several other family members are present while your subject reads.
2. A child gives no clues, verbal or behavioral, that he heard a remark directed to him.
3. A child is attending to a conversation in which he is not involved. Code his behavior as AT, while those he is attending to would be coded NR.

Examples of Non-NR:

1. Father, while reading the paper, is asked by his wife to let the dog out. He looks up for a brief moment, then returns to his reading. Code IG.

RC (RECEIVE): Use this category when a person receives an object from another person or is touched physically by a person and is passively showing no response to the contact. If the person touched responds in some way, then the specific response should be coded rather than RC.

Examples of RC:

1. Child sits quietly while mother combs her hair.
2. A child remains passive after being hugged by another family member.
3. A son shows no response when father puts his arm around him.

Examples of Non-RC:

1. Parent pats child on head and child returns an approving smile. Child's response to the pat would be coded AP rather than coding the passive behavior of RC.

TH (TOUCH): Use of this behavior code indicates non-verbal passing of objects or neutral non-verbal physical contact.

Examples of TH:

1. Father silently passes newspaper to mother. Code father TH, mother RC, as no verbal comments were offered.
2. The neutral picking up of a small child for no apparent reason.
3. A small child puts his hand on someone's arm. No other overt behavior is occurring.

Examples of Non-TH:
1. Mother picks up small child, places him in high chair, and states her intention to feed him. Code this WK rather than TH because of her intention to feed him.

Second-Order Verbal and Non-Verbal Behaviors (SS)

SS (SELF-STIMULATION): Use of this code is for a narrow class of behaviors which the individual does to or for himself and cannot be coded by any other codes.

Example of SS:
1. A child bounces and/or rocks his body.
2. A child lies on the floor, feels a blanket, and sucks a thumb.
3. A person sits and pulls out his hair, eyelashes, or bites his nails.

Examples of Non-SS:
1. Child's continuous foot-tapping at an audible level, which is distracting to others around him, would be coded TE if it appeared to be an obvious attempt to disrupt those persons.

How to Use the Code System

Each family member is the subject of at least five minutes of observation during each session. During each five-minute period of time, the interactions between the subject and the other family members are recorded every six seconds. The interactions are recorded on a behavior rating sheet (see Appendix 1). Each rating sheet has five six-second intervals on each line; therefore, each line represents 30 seconds. There are 10 lines on each sheet, thereby creating a total of five minutes for each sheet. The observer is signaled at the end of each 30-second interval by an auditory signal emitted from a clipboard used to hold the behavior rating sheets.

Numbering Family Members

Family members are given numbers from 1 to 8; 1 is always the deviant child; 2 is always the father; 3 always the mother; 4 always the second deviant child or the oldest child in the family, whichever is applicable. Other siblings are assigned numbers in ascending order, according to age, oldest to youngest. If there are more than six children in a family, the designation of A, B, C, and so on is used for the additional children following coded child #8. (Example: nine children in a family would be 1, 4, 5, 6, 7, 8, A, B, C.). The number 9 is used to indicate occasions when more than two people are responding to a subject's behavior. The number 0 is reserved for the designation of the observer; occasionally a subject will direct behavior to the observer. The observer's behavior must be coded as well as the behavior of the family member; therefore, 0 is used to differentiate the observer from the rest of the family. If another person is in the home on a temporary basis, we assign him/her the number 8 and note on our profile who it is (example: grandmother, aunt).

Each six-second interval must include a number designating the subject, a code abbreviation descriptive of the subject's behavior, a number designating the respondent(s), and a code designating the behavior of the respondent(s). For the purpose of this manual, a respondent is any person who is noted as reacting to the subject of the observation. For example, the father (subject) tells his son to turn down the stereo and the child does so. The six-second frame on the rating sheet will look like this: 2CM 1CO . The 2 designates father, CM indicates that he gave a command, 1 indicates the CM was directed to the son, and CO indicates the son's response.

In coding family interaction, the pattern of observation usually follows this progression: the subject emits a behavior(s) which is followed by a response from at least one other person in that environment. The observer therefore would first look at the subject, note what he was doing, and code that behavior in the appropriate frame on the coding sheet. The observer would then note the response(s) of the other family members to the subject's behavior, and code their responses following those of the subject. The observer would then return to the subject and code his next behavior and follow it again by the responses of other family members. Pictorially, the observation sequence would look like this: S–R S–R S–R where S = subject # and behavior emitted, and R = respondent's # and behaviors emitted.

On occasion, other family members' behavior may be coded first as their behavior precedes the subject's in time. For example, if the son is the subject and the father tells him to take out the garbage, the command of the father would precede whatever behavior the son did in relation to the command. In this case, father's command would be coded first (2CM), followed immediately by the child's response (possibly 1CO or 1NC). The full six-second frame would therefore be coded 2CM 1CO .

The one rule we do follow in coding sequences is that each new behavior coding sheet must *begin* with the subject being coded first. This rule prevents the observer from accidentally following the behavior of the wrong family member for that sheet. Each coding sheet will represent one specific family member as the subject of that five-minute segment.

Double Coding

Double coding is attributing two behaviors to one person. For example, mother says to son, "Put your tee shirt on. I don't like you coming to the table in your bare skin." Mother's behavior is coded 3CMDI since a reasonable request was made and the mother indicates disapproval of the son. The respondent can also be double-coded; for example, son says, "Okay, get off my back," and reaches for his tee shirt. Code this 1CO NE. Thus, the completed six-second frame on the coding sheet will look like this: 3CMDI 1CONE .

Z Coding

Z coding is the coding of one or two responses from two separate respondents at the same time. Often, more than one person responds to the subject's behavior. If two people respond, you should code both persons, identified by their numbers, and the proper behavior each emitted. The response can be the same behavior, for example, code 4/5TA when two siblings simultaneously answer the subject. When the two respondents react differently, then the coding can look like this: 4TA 5DI. In this instance, one sibling talked and the other was critical of your subject. The maximum number of reactions to the subject that can be coded in any rating frame is four. This occurs when two separate respondents are each double-coded. An example would be: 3WK TA 4WK DI. In this example of two respondents, mother is working and talking about other than the work situation and a sibling is working and disapproving in response to the subject's behavior. When writing codes on the behavior rating sheet, the letter Z can be used as one would the symbol + (plus) to link the two respondents' behavior(s) as simultaneous responses to your subject. Using the example stated above, suppose you are observing a kitchen scene where your subject is playing at the kitchen table while her mother is drying dishes and talking to a sibling who is in turn drying dishes and verbally disapproving of the subject's play behavior. A six-second coded representation of this scene would be: 1PL 3WK TA Z 4WK DI.[1] Z coding of the subject can never take place because you are to target only *one* subject at a time.

Using Numeric Code 9

If *three or more persons* are responding to the subject at the same time and their responses are in the form of identical behavior, the number 9 is assigned to precede the specific behavior code. For example, if the subject and at least three family members are playing a card game together, their behaviors may be represented by the sequence 1PL 9PL .

When respondents are exhibiting *different* behaviors at the same time, the observer must choose the most relevant respondents (relevant in terms of their apparent effect on the subject's behavior) and code their responses to the subject. For example, if the subject and three family members are playing a game and one family member tells the subject to get up and let the dog in, rather than coding 1PL 9PL, you would code 4CM 1CO. Observers must also remember the rule that first-order behaviors take precedence over second-order behaviors (see page 21). If, in a group activity, one respondent emits a first-order behavior while other members are emitting second-order behaviors, the first order behavior *must* be coded.

In coding, the observer must have complete sequences in each frame; an identifying number for the subject; the subject's behavior; an identifying number for the respondent, and his behavior.

---

1. In practice, Z is most often omitted because of limitations of space and time. The real utility of the Z is for the keypunch format. *Only respondent's behavior can be Z coded.*

Sequences that are repeated on a line need not be coded using numbers and letters over and over again. Instead, simply put a dash and a slash (i.e., "—/") in subsequent frames to indicate that the same interaction reoccurred. Never use these symbols at the beginning of a line even though the sequence is the same as those in the preceding lines. Always write out the first sequence of a line and then the use of the dash and slash as is appropriate (i.e., 1TA 9NR —/ —/ —/ —/).

Special Applications

In two-member families, don't use the number 9 at all (example, mother-child family). In three-member families, if *non-directive* behaviors (example: WK, PL, NO) are consequated by NR, code respondents with the identification number 9 rather than the specific numbers usually assigned to individual members. In families of *more than three* persons, the general rules for application of code 9 still stand.

Coding Animals

Animals are not coded using our observation system. Should your subject play with or talk to a pet, the subject's behavior would be coded as it occurred. The response to your subject's behavior would be coded as the responses from other *humans* in the immediate environment.

Example:

> Johnny plays with his pet dog while his parents are attending to other matters. This interaction would be coded 1PL 9NR as no humans responded to Johnny. Should any family member emit any behavior towards an animal, it should be coded as either TA or PL (whichever appears closest to appropriate representation). Use of other codes would result in incomplete chains being coded. For example, if mother commands the dog to do something and we don't code dog's behavior, our CM would not be followed by a CO or NC, thus giving us faulty data on family interaction.

Interruptions in Observation

During an observation, disruptions may occur. There are several events that can occur and, because of these events, a series of symbols besides the behavioral categories have been devised to record in a simple fashion what those events are. If the observer takes a break *while* coding a line, then the point at which the break occurred is coded with a letter "U." If the subject takes a break while he is being coded *within* a line, the observer writes the letter "K" at that point where the subject took a break. Examples of the subject taking a break are leaving the room during an observation or being out of view of the observer for one reason or another. If the observer break occurs at the *end* of a line, the letter "B" is used; if the subject break occurs at the *end* of a line, the letter "A" is used. The symbols "A," "B," "K," and "U" are to be circled on the Behavioral Rating Sheet so that they are clearly discernible from the behavior codes. When a break has occurred in the middle of a line, the observer has two options. After the break, resume coding on the same line or wait until the next signal and begin a new line. If you resume coding on the same line, when remaining frames are full, mark an observer break (B), wait for the next signal, and begin the next line.

At the end of the rating sheet, lines are provided for the observer to record the situation that was going on while the subject was being observed. The observer should write terse statements or simply one-word descriptions of what was occurring, e.g., dinner, working in the kitchen, reading a newspaper, etc. When more than one descriptive statement is used, the observer should write in the line the number or numbers appropriate to each statement. Also, any event that occurred that was difficult to code should be included so the observer can obtain clarification on how the action should be coded.

Data Collection Procedures

Observation Setting Rules

During each observation, the family must adhere to a certain set of rules. These rules have been developed in order to facilitate the data collection procedures and to provide a standardized observational setting. We have found these rules must be made very clear to the clients. It is useful to give the family a typed list of the observation rules and to provide frequent reminders in order to reduce

confusion and missed sessions.
1. Everyone in the family must be present.
2. No guests.
3. The family is limited to two rooms.
4. The observer(s) will wait only 10 minutes for all to be present.
5. Telephone: No calls out; incoming calls answered *briefly*.
6. No TV.
7. No talking by family to observer(s) while coding.
8. Family may not discuss *anything* with observer(s) that relates to their problems or the procedures they are using to deal with them.

Observer Preparation

Before arrival in the client's home, the observer must prepare the rating sheets. One rating sheet is used for each family member for each five-minute period. The total number of sheets per observation for each family member is determined by the particular clinical or research needs. For example, during baseline, two sheets of data are collected on each family member. Collection of data requires that each rating sheet be identified clearly. In the "subject" blank, the observer puts down the appropriate number of the person who is the subject of the observation. In the "observer" blank, the observer puts his or her initials. In the "date" blank, the observer writes in the number of the current month, day, and year. In the "sheet no." blank, the observer records the number of the sheet to be used for that particular subject, i.e., if it is the first five minutes that the subject is being observed, number "1" is placed in the blank, and so on. At the top of each rating sheet are ID number blanks (see Figure 1, page 34). This can be completed after the observation.

After numbering and labeling the rating sheets as described above, take all the "sheet number 1's" (i.e., the first sheet for each family member) and place them in random order. The same sequence is repeated for the second sheet for each family member. Each time an observation is done, the sheets need to be randomly ordered. Each family member is the subject of observation in the order in which the sheets have been placed.

Key Punching

From the behavior rating sheet, the data are keypunched according to the format in Figure 2, proofed, edited, and formed into computer files for subsequent computer assisted analyses. Information registered in columns 1 through 19 is the same as that recorded at the top of the Behavior Rating Sheet in the ID number blank.

Figure 2

OREGON SOCIAL LEARNING CENTER

Family Observational Data
Keypunch Format

Card Col.	Data Description	Code
1 – 2	Family number	2 digit family ID
3 – 4	Data type	'03'
5 – 10	Date	Mo/da/yr
11	Subject number of target subject for this segment	Ex: 1 for deviant child
12	Phase	1 digit code
13 – 14	Subphase	2 digit code
15	Observer number	
16 – 17	Therapist	
18	Sheet number	1,2,3,..., A, B, C,...
19	Card number	1, 2, 3,..., A, B, C,...
21 – 26	1st behavior	Ex: IATTAZ
27 – 32	2nd behavior	Ex: IATTAZ
33 – 38	3rd behavior	Ex: IATTAZ
39 – 44	4th behavior	Ex: IATTAZ
45 – 50	5th behavior	Ex: IATTAZ
51 – 56	6th behavior	Ex: IATTAZ
57 – 62	7th behavior	Ex: IATTAZ
63 – 68	8th behavior	Ex: IATTAZ
69 – 74	9th behavior	Ex: IATTAZ
75 – 80	10th behavior	Ex: IATTAZ

Sample Observation

To illustrate the use of the behavioral code, a fictional description of a family interaction is provided. This scene is typical of actual observations. The subject of this rating sheet is mother, #3; Mark, age 9, #1, is the deviant

FIGURE 1

SAMPLE OBSERVATION
BEHAVIOR RATING SHEET

ID Number [ ]

Sheet No. _1_

Subject _Mother #3_   Observer _BG_   Date _4-13-75_

#					
1	3WK-9NR	———/	———/	3CM-4NC WK WH	3WK-9NR
2	4DP-3CO	3WK-4WK	———/	3WK-4WK TA TA	3WK-4WK
3	3CM-1NC	3WK-9NR	———/	3WK-2NR TA	———/
4	3WK-2NR TA	———/	3CN-1CO	3DI-1NE	3WK-9NR
5	3WK-2AT	———/	3CM-2CO	3WK-2WK	———/
6	3WK-2WK	2TA-3TA	———/	3WK-9NR	———/ ⓑ
7	3AT-¼NR	———/	———/	1YE-3IG	3WK-9NR
8	3WK-4WK	———/	———/	3WK-4WK 1 AT	3WK-¼WK
9	3WK-¼WK	1TE-3DI	1HU-3IG	3WK-¼WK	———/
10	3WK-¼WK	3CN-1CO PN	3WK-4WK	———/	———/

child; father, #2; and Susan, age 14, #4.

Scene opens. Mother is cooking dinner, father is nearby reading a newspaper. Mark is playing with a car close to father, and Susan is standing near the sink, looking at the dishes left from breakfast. The observer begins to code as mother works silently cutting vegetables. This continues for 18 seconds, or three frames (3WK 9NR). Mother says, "Okay, Susan, get going on those dishes" (3CMWK). Susan, in a high, nasal voice, replies, "Look, they are all gucky with grease!" and continues to gaze at the sink (4WH NC). Mother goes on working with the vegetables. Susan says to mother, "You come and get the greasy water out for me" (4 DP). Mother quietly goes over, begins to prepare the sink for Susan (3CO). Mother puts hot water and soap in the sink while Susan helps. Susan washes and mother rinses (3WK 4WK for 12 seconds). Mother asks, "Did you get to school on time this morning?" (3TA WK). Susan answers, "Yes" (4WK TA). Dishwashing continues (3WK 4WK). Mother speaks to Mark, "Mark, come and dry the dishes" (3CM). Mark continues playing (1NC). Mother returns to cutting vegetables (3WK 9NR for 12 seconds). Mother then talks to father about weekend plans as she works (3WK TA). Father is engrossed in the paper (2NR). This one-sided conversation goes on for 24 seconds (3WK TA 2NR). Mother turns her attention to Mark, saying sharply, "Mark, you immediately come dry these dishes!" (3CN). Mark jumps up to dry dishes (1CO). Mother complains, "You know drying dishes is your chore and I don't like the way you have been trying to get out of it" (3DI). Mark says, "You're bugging me again" (1NE). Mother goes back to cutting vegetables (3WK 9NR). Father looks up from his newspaper, watches mother (3WK 2AT for 12 seconds). Mother asks father to open a jar lid (3CM). Father opens jar (2CO), sets it aside, picks up another knife, helps mother cut vegetables (3WK 2WK for 18 seconds). Vegetables are finished. Father says to mother, "Let's go to Portland..." etc., and discusses weekend plans (2TA 3TA for 12 seconds). Mother begins to assemble dinner (3WK). Father picks up newspaper again (9NR). Mark leaves the room to go to the bathroom. Observer stops coding, marks a B. Mark returns, buzzer sounds, observer resumes coding. Mark picks up drying dishes. Susan and he start quarreling. Mother watches for 18 seconds (3AT 1/4NR).

Mark yells, "Mother!" (1YE). Mother turns away (3IG) and resumes cooking (3WK 9NR). Susan finishes her part of the dishes and comes to help mother with dinner (3WK 4WK for 18 seconds). There is some talk but it is about the dinner preparation. Mark comes to watch his sister and mother (3WK 4WK Z 1AT for six seconds). Mark teases mother by dangling food close to her face (1TE). Mother responds, "I'm not in the mood for that, young man!" (3DI). Mark retorts, "You are a dumb old grouch!" (1HU). Mother moves away silently (3IG). All resume working together (3WK 1/4WK for 18 seconds). Mark turns to Susan, throws a piece of vegetable at Susan. Mother grabs Mark's arm, pushes him toward a chair angrily, saying, "Get on that chair, now!" (3CN PN 1CO). Mother and Susan continue preparing dinner (3WK 4WK for 18 seconds). End of rating sheet.

Index of Behavioral Code Definitions

Code		Page
AP	Approval	25
AT	Attention	28
CM	Command	22
CN	Command Negative	22
CO	Compliance	25
CR	Cry	23
DI	Disapproval	25
DP	Dependency	26
DS	Destructiveness	23
HR	High Rate	24
HU	Humiliate	23
IG	Ignore	26
IN	Indulgence	27
LA	Laugh	23
NC	Non-compliance	27
NE	Negativism	23
NO	Normative	29
NR	No Response	29
PL	Play	27
PN	Physical Negative	24
PP	Physical Positive	24
RC	Receive	29
SS	Self-stimulation	30
TA	Talk	28
TE	Tease	28
TH	Touch	29
WH	Whine	23
WK	Work	28
YE	Yell	23

First Order Verbal Behaviors
 (CM, CN, CR, HU, LA, NE, WH, YE) 22
First Order Non-Verbal Behaviors
 (DS, HR, PN, PP) 23
First Order Verbal or Non-Verbal Behaviors
 (AP, CO, DI, DP, IG, IN, NC, PL, TE, WK) 25

Second Order Verbal Behaviors (TA) 28
Second Order Non-Verbal Behaviors
 (AT, NO, NR, RC, TH, SS) 28
Second Order Verbal and
 Non-Verbal Behaviors (SS) 30

Chapter 5

Procedures for Training Observers

S. L. Maerov, B. Brummett, and J. B. Reid

The purpose of this chapter is to outline the steps necessary for learning the coding system and using it correctly. Each step is important and must be mastered before proceeding to the next.

Step One: Reread Chapter IV. Before attempting to memorize the code abbreviations and definitions, trainees should familiarize themselves with the general concept of naturalistic observation. A quick reading of Chapter IV with emphasis on the second section, "How to Use the Code System," should facilitate this process. A set of review questions for training observers have been provided on page 39.

Step Two: Memorize code abbreviations and definitions. Once Chapter IV is mastered, the behavior code abbreviations and their definitions *must* be committed to memory. It is best to construct a set of flash cards carrying the code abbreviation on one side and the behavioral definition or example situation described on the other side of the card. Working alone or in groups, the trainees can take turns matching definitions to codes or reciting definitions in order to become competent in applying the code system.

Step Three: Practice writing the code abbreviations. Trainees should now practice writing the code abbreviations on the coding sheet. At this point in the program, the video tapes of family interaction (available from Oregon Social Learning Center) are introduced and observers begin the process of applying codes to units of observed behavior.

It is suggested that trainees practice behavioral discrimination in their own environment. This can be done by coding TV commercials (usually 30 seconds in length), television scenes, or thinking code abbreviations while observing the occurrence of the various behaviors in one's own interaction with others.

Every attempt should be made by the trainee to use the code in such a manner that it tells the truth, i.e., the coding reflects as closely as possible the specific behavioral occurrences in the situation.

Observers at the Oregon Social Learning Center (OSLC) have been trained both individually and in groups of two to 10 people. Initial training sessions are usually not more than one hour in duration. At times, two sessions a day, morning and afternoon, have been scheduled. As trainees become more familiar with the coding process, increasing amounts of time are spent on rules and special coding situations.

In addition to observer tape and live training, the trainee attends regularly scheduled observer meetings. Observer meetings at OSLC are held weekly. These sessions cover any coding questions arising for any observer. Questions for discussion during observer training sessions are provided on page 39. Periodically, the observers reclarify behavioral definitions by re-reading and discussing the coding chapter. In addition, video-tapes are employed to assess both observer drift and reliability.

The average time required before a trainee is competent and therefore ready for field experience is 15 to 20 hours of practice with video tapes. Experience has shown that one-hour sessions can, as trainees progress, be lengthened to an hour and one-half, and then to two hours.

As skills develop, the trainee codes longer intervals until s/he is coding a full five-minute session. This is later extended until the trainee is capable of coding up to one hour of consecutive interaction. Reliability is checked at various intervals during training (A publication describing reliability and complexity scoring methods is available from OSLC). No major emphasis is placed on reliability during the first week of training. Past experience has suggested that skill, speed, and reliability develop together with practice.

During the second week, the trainee should check his or her reliability on at least two five-minute coding sheets and score 80% reliability with the observer trainer or the precoded observation sheets. The trainee is then ready for further training in a home setting with an experienced, reliable observer.

In field assignment, the observer trainee on the first home visit observes and acquaints her/himself with the home situation (i.e., identifies family members by number and name and becomes familiar with the rooms in which the observation is to take place). The observer is not expected to code for reliability in this initial trial. The first home observation is meant to be an introduction to family interaction. To become "reliable," the trainee must achieve an inter-observer agreement rate of at least 75% on two consecutive observations, with a reliable observer in the home. Each of these reliabilities must be met with a different calibrator. This latter criterion is particular to the Oregon Social Learning Center.

Questions will, of course, be raised in the home setting concerning coding. It is strongly encouraged that these questions be talked over *after* the observers have returned to the office.

Because naturalistic home observations are often more complex than those observed from video-tapes, the trainee will not maintain as high a reliability in the first attempts at coding *in vivo*. Practice in the field is the only prescription and several trials may be needed to meet criterion.

Observer Conduct

One of the first and most enduring contacts a client has at the Oregon Social Learning Center is with the observer. With this in mind, the following standards have been developed for observer conduct.

It is recommended that conversations with clients should be of short duration and about neutral subjects. All requests from clients for advice should be referred to the therapist. Observers are often asked to have dinner or to have coffee; these offers should be refused in a firm, yet friendly manner.

An observer is not a therapist and all observers should be instructed never to assume this role. A friendly but professional attitude is required, one that can reassure clients but does not intrude upon their problems.

Client privacy is of extreme importance. The home environment is one of the last bastions left to a family and, therefore, needs to be highly respected. All information gleaned—both informal impressions and formal data collected—is in the strictest sense held confidential. A non-judgmental and factual accounting should characterize the data collection process. As families progress through baseline, intervention, and follow-up, this impartial observer attitude develops trust in the team approach of the Oregon Social Learning Center. Clients learn that observers are as quick to report positive behaviors and successes as they are negative behaviors and failures. Observers should use the last name of the client in the client's home, but refer to these families by the child's first name and family initial when discussing them within the project (e.g., the Terry C. family).

Observers should be aware of the need to dress appropriately. Clients come from various backgrounds, both socially and economically, and care should be taken that no offense is given. Casual sport-type clothing is adequate, but jeans, cut-offs, or halter tops should not be worn; similarly, overdressing should be avoided.

An assignment to a home observation begins by completing the coding sheets with the proper I.D. This should be done in the office. Care should be taken that the clipboard timer is functioning properly. The observer should arrive on time and briefly introduce her/himself if s/he has not been there before. If this is the first observation for a family, it is often valuable for the observer to spend a brief period allowing the children and parents to examine the clipboard and hear the "beeps." The observer should explain that s/he cannot talk while working and check which rooms are in the coding area. S/he may also briefly review the observation requirements. The rules listed below must be explicitly followed during every observation.

1. Everyone in the family must be present.
2. No guests.
3. The family is limited to two rooms.
4. The observers will wait only 10 minutes for all to be present in the two rooms.
5. Telephone: No calls out; briefly answer incoming calls.
6. No TV.
7. No talking to observers while they are coding.
8. Families may not discuss *anything* with observer(s) that relates to their problems or the procedures being used to deal with them.

While coding, the observer should give no facial or body cues to his/her subjects. Tracking and coding a subject should be done as unobtrusively as possible. Observers code both sitting and standing up (sometimes while walking). The objective is to see and code the subject adequately. All breaks in the sequential flow of data should be entered. If the observer becomes confused, timing out of sequence, or other similar difficulties, an observer break should be taken. *It is always better to lose data than to code inaccurately!*

Questions for Discussion During Observer Training Sessions

Reliability and Drift
Observer Bias
Complexity
Coding Rules and Procedures
Code Definitions and Examples

Review Questions for Observer Training

The following section contains a series of questions for review and discussion. The purpose of this section is to help observers and trainees gain a better basic understanding of the intricacies in naturalistic observation. Answers should be recorded on separate sheets. Correct as well as incorrect answers should be discussed within the group. Keep essay answers brief and to the point.

The following questins cover the material presented in chapters 2 through 5. An answer key is provided on page 42.

Reliability and Drift

1. Parental reports tend to accurately represent how their children act when at home.
   T   F

2. Different interviewers may obtain very different information from the same set of parents.   T   F

3. The lack of research support for the validity of parents' global judgments about their child has given strength to the need for observational procedures and measures.
   T   F

4. Mothers and fathers see their children's traits as very similar.   T   F

5. Parents have a bias to report improvement in the behavior of problem children when no observable changes have occurred.
   T   F

6. Reliability has been shown to vary as a function of subjects, sex, personality characteristics, complexity of the code and even socio-economic status.   T   F

7. Observers should meet once per month to recalibrate and discuss problems in observation.   T   F

8. The tendency for observers to gradually change their use of the observation codes is called _____.

9. Observers may have high inter-observer agreement yet have low agreement levels when compared to precoded tapes.
   T   F

10. In the Social Learning Project, every _____ home observation during baseline, and every _____ thereafter is attended by two observers.

11. Observer drift must be prevented through _____
_____

12. Groups of observers are susceptible to _____ _____.

13. When two observers attend and observe the same scene for the purpose of doing a reliability check, one observer is called the _____.

14. Percentage agreement between observers is calculated by the following formula:

15. A frame is defined as a _____ second time sample of behavior.

16. A frame is divided into _____ parts: the _____ number and antecedent behavior and the _____ number and consequation.

17. Observer agreement involves full agreement within an observation frame.   T   F

Observer Bias

1. Experimenters' or therapists' expectancies do not affect, to a significant degree, the data collected by well-trained observers.
   T   F

2. The act of giving monitors feedback concerning their decline in levels of agreement will produce a return to higher levels of agreement for a lengthy period of time.
   T   F

Complexity

1. Reliability drops/rises/remains unaffected as the complexity of the interaction increases.

Coding Observed Behaviors

1. The present Family Interaction Coding System was designed primarily to describe _____ behaviors, together with the antecedents and consequences which follow them.

2. Observers may code two subjects simultaneously when using the FICS.
   T   F

3. Every 20 seconds, the observer receives an auditory signal from his/her clipboard.
   T   F

4. The observer may begin writing on any line on the coding sheet and progress to the next line when s/he feels it is appropriate.
   T   F

5. Each family member is the subject of at least _____ minutes of observation during each session.

6. Each line on the observation sheet represents _____ seconds.

7. Each page of coding represents what length of time? _____.

8. What number is the target child in the family assigned? _____.

9. Siblings in a family are assigned numbers in _____ order.

10. Siblings are assigned order for coding according to what criterion? _____

11. Nine children in a family would be numbered in what fashion? _____

12. The number _____ is used when there are three or more people responding to a subject's behavior.

13. The number _____ is used to designate the observer.

14. Persons temporarily in the home during the observation period are assigned the number _____.

15. On what occasions may other family members' behavior be coded before the subject's? _____

16. *Rule.* Any new behavior coding sheet must begin with the subject being coded first.
    T   F

17. Define double-coding. Give an example of double-coding. _____

18. Z coding is the coding of one or two responses from the same person at different points in time.   T   F

19. When respondents are exhibiting *different* behaviors at the same time, the observer must choose the most relevant respondents and code their responses to the subject.   T   F

20. Observers must remember that _____ order behaviors take precedence over _____ order behaviors when coding.

21. In a group activity, if one respondent emits a first-order behavior while other mem-

bers are emitting second-order behaviors, the _____ order behavior must be coded first.

22. Observer breaks while coding are signalled on the coding sheet by the letters _____.

23. List the specific codes used to signal breaks in activity while coding. State the reasons for each code. _____
_____
_____
_____

24. Families are allowed to watch TV during observations, but only if the volume is low enough for the observer to hear family members talking.   T   F

25. What problems can arise from having unstructured observation sessions?
_____
_____
_____

Behavioral Definition Questions

1. Family members are eating; only father is drinking coffee. Mother notices that his cup is empty, stops feeding the baby, gets up, and refills his cup. Code mother as _____.

2. Two siblings having an ongoing conversation about the day's activities. Code as _____.

3. Mother grabs a child's arm and shoves the child. Code as _____.

4. "I give up. No matter what I do, I can't do it. I can try 100 times, but I can't get it. You can show me all you want, but I can't." Code as _____.

5. When a person uses a slurring, nasal, or high-pitched voice, use this category. The content of the statement can be of an approving, disapproving, or neutral quality. The main element is the voice quality. This is the definition for _____.

6. "Johnny, it's time to pick up your toys." Code as _____.

7. Running back and forth repeatedly in the living room. Code as _____.

8. Smiles, head nods. Code as _____.

9. "I don't like that dress," "You didn't pick up your clothes again this morning." Code as _____.

10. Coloring or drawing a picture. Code as _____.

11. In a sing-song voice, one child says to another, "You got in trouble and I didn't." Code as _____.

12. Use of this code is for a narrow class of behaviors which the individual does to or for himself and cannot be coded by any other codes. The code is _____.

13. A small child puts his hand on someone's arm. No other overt behavior is occurring. Code this _____.

14. School-related activities, hobbies, music practice. Code this _____.

15. Child touches mother and asks a question. Mother turns away or walks away. Code mother _____.

16. "Stop that *right* now!" Code as _____.

17. "You dumb old grouch!" (Said in a derogatory fashion.) Code as _____.

18. A hug, a pat, a kiss. Code this _____.

Answer Key to Questions for Observer Training

Reliability and Drift

1. F   2. T   3. T   4. F   5. T   6. T   7. F   8. observer drift   9. T   10. third, fourth   11. Frequent reliability checks, recalibration on standard video tapes, sample complex as well as simple interactions during reliability checks.   12. observer drift   13. calibrator

14. $$\frac{\text{number of frames of agreement}}{\text{number of frames agreement} + \text{number of frames of disagreement}}$$

15. six   16. two, subject's, respondent's   17. F

Observer Bias

1. T   2. T

Complexity

1. drops

Coding Observed Behaviors

1. aggressive   2. F   3. F   4. F   5. five   6. thirty   7. five minutes   8. one   9. ascending   10. age   11. 1, 4, 5, 6, 7, 8, A, B, C   12. nine   13. zero   14. eight   15. When their behavior precedes the behavior of the subject in time.   16. T   17. Double coding is attributing two behaviors to one person. 3CMDI / 1CONE.   18. F   19. T   20. first, second   21. first   22. U and B.

23. 1) U — observer takes a break while coding a line.
    2) K — subject takes a break while s/he is being coded *within* a line.
    3) A — if a subject break occurs at the *end* of a line.
    4) B — if an observer break occurs at the *end* of a line.

24. F   25. Family members can keep from interacting with each other.

Behavioral Definition Questions

1. IN   2. TA / TA   3. PN   4. NE   5. WH   6. CM   7. HR   8. AP   9. DI   10. PL   11. TE   12. SS   13. TH   14. WK   15. IG   16. CN   17. HU   18. PP

Chapter 6

The Development of Specialized Observational Systems

John B. Reid
Oregon Social Learning Center

The observational coding system described in the present volume was designed to be multipurpose in nature. We needed a system which would be useful for the evaluation of treatment in terms of broad summary type data (e.g., Total Deviant Behavior, Total Targeted Behavior); and we needed a system which would provide fine-grained sequential data describing the behavioral interchanges among family members in order to carry out tests of theoretical hypotheses about the development and maintenance of aggressive behavior patterns in the family setting. Finally, we needed a system which lent itself to the evaluation of hypotheses concerning the observational process, data stability, reliability and validity.

It is probably the case that many who read the current volume simply do not need an observational system as complex and flexible as the one presented here. For example, if the prospective user wishes only to evaluate the outcome of treatment in terms of pre, post and follow-up levels of social aggression in the family setting, then a system which allows for sequential analyses of interchanges is not necessary. Since, over the past number of years, many clinicians interested in our system wanted it for only one purpose — the evaluation and monitoring of treatment — this chapter will be devoted to trying to explain how one might go about devising and evaluating an observational system which is tailor-made to specialized needs. As will become apparent, it is possible to devise a simple, efficient observational system which has sufficiently solid psychometric characteristics to provide useful data on outcome effectiveness (at least on the day-to-day observable level). First, a set of general principles will be discussed; and second, some example coding systems will be outlined. Third, procedures for insuring data quality (reliability and validity) will be described.

1. *General principles and ideas underlying the design of a specialized observational system.*

The first question you should ask yourself is, "Why do we want an observational code?" For an observational system to be useful, the user must be interested in data on day-to-day observable behavior. The more behavioral the orientation, the easier it will be to construct a code. For example, it is easier to observe and record temper tantrums or words spoken than it is to record instances of ego strength or positive self concept. If one deals with selectively mute children, it is easier to develop a system to measure how many times the child speaks to others than it is to measure the anxiety the child feels in social interactions. Thus, the first consideration in developing a behavioral coding system is whether or not the outcome variables of interest can be translated into observable and objective code categories. All this means is: can two people, who watch a subject simultaneously and independently, agree on when an instance of a given code category occurs? The first step, then, is to decide what characteristic(s) is to be measured, and to translate it into potentially observable categories. Some examples of this process are given below:

What you are really interested in measuring	*Possible translations into code categories*
1. Shyness (does the child come out of his/her shell as a function of treatment?)	Rate or frequency of verbal initiations to others. Frequency of playful interchanges with others. Amount of time spent with peers or sibs compared with time spent with adults. Frequency of boistrous (laughing, rough-housing, etc.) activities with others.
2. Abuse (does the parent relate in a less physical and coercive manner with his/her children as the result of treatment?)	Frequency of threats to children. Frequency of negative physical contacts. Frequency of yelling at children. Frequency of playful interactions. Frequency of positive comments to children.
3. Depression (is the client less depressed after treatment?)	Frequency of initiations to others. Frequency of task behaviors (doing work rather than sitting or lying on the couch). Frequency of self depricating or 'poor me' statements. Frequency of weeping.
4. Aggressiveness (is the client less hostile towards others as a result of treatment?	Frequency of Total Deviant Behaviors used in the code previously described.

Given that one is able to find behavioral examples which reflect an important characteristic of the client, the next step is to find out if they are realistic. Basically, this boils down to three things: can two people agree when the behavioral events occur? Do the behaviors actually occur when observers are present? Do the observations show differences between known groups, e.g., do known abusive parents show fewer positive initiations and playful interactions with their child than parents who do not have that referral problem? Some categories are highly reliable, make excellent sense, and would undoubtedly differentiate between abusive and non-abusive parents. However, the observer is never going to see them (e.g., hitting the children with blunt instruments, or otherwise injuring the child). The key to finding out whether categories are realistic is to go out into the target setting and take a look.

If, for example, one is interested in the observation of shyness in children, the first step is to create a list of possible categories. The second step is to make a few visits to the homes of shy children presently being seen. Sit in the home and try to write a narrative account of what the child does during a half hour period. Try not to include descriptions of motivation or intent in the narrative, as those sorts of things are extremely difficult to record in a reliable fashion. Thus, keep the statements simple and behavioral. After making a few of these observations, one is able to see if the initial categories are adequate. If one is extremely lucky, most of the narrative statements recorded during the first few observations will fit nicely into the initial categories devised. If one has the type of experience we usually have when setting out to develop a code, then the categories will have to be reconsidered and revised after the first few narrative accounts are studied. To summarize the steps to this point: (1) devise a tentative list of observable categories; (2) collect a few narrative accounts of the behavior of the target clients; (3) examine the narrative accounts to see how many behavioral statements can be coded in terms of the tentative list of categories; (4) revise the list of categories so that most of the relevant narrative statements may be coded. After creating a revised list of categories, go back into the homes of a few clients and try to code the subjects' behavior in terms of those categories.

As with all measuring devices used in social science, it is extremely important to standardize as much as possible the situation in which data are gathered. One should decide in advance: (1) the time(s) of day the data are to be gathered; (2) the location(s) in which observations are to be made; (3) who should participate as targets of observations: and (4) methods for reducing interruptions. See pages 30–33 for possible operating rules. It is also important to decide on length and frequency of observations. We have found that one hour sessions are workable, and that an absolute minimum of two sessions at each assessment phase (e.g., pre-treatment, post treatment, follow-up) are needed to insure data quality. Once these working rules are formulated, they must be applied in the same manner to each family for the development and assessment of the observation system itself.

Once the coding system has been constructed and the rules of observation have been set, the next step is to assess observer reliability. This, as well as other analytical steps will be discussed after some examples of coding systems have been given.

The Critical Incident System

How should behavior be recorded? Although there are many possible formats that might be employed, one straight forward strategy will be presented here: the critical incident system.

In this type of system, one simply records a relevant set of actions each time they occur. If no instance of the behavioral categories occurs, then nothing is recorded. Before giving concrete examples of how such a recording system may be devised, the major shortcoming of this system will be described. The main problem we've encountered with the critical incident system is that observers tend to nod off between critical incidents and to miss them when they occur. Suppose that the behaviors of interest happen once every two minutes or so. It is likely that the observer will become bored with the task after several observations. If this happens, the vigilance of the observer will decrease, which in turn increases the probability that the events, when they do occur, will be missed. If the behaviors happen at a relatively high rate, say every 10-15 seconds, this vigilance problem should be negligible.

Example 1. Suppose that one is interested in a behavioral coding system for evaluating aggressive behavior in the home setting. Suppose further that the sequence of aggressive behaviors is not of interest, only their frequency or rate. Finally, suppose that the reactions of other family members to the child's aggressiveness are not of interest. After starting with an initial list of categories, which has been modified on the basis of narrative behavioral accounts taken in the homes of several clients, the behavioral categories are as follows: Negative Physical Contacts (NP); Crying (C); Threatening (T); Destroying Things (DT); Yelling (Y); Non-compliance (NC) and Roughhousing (RH). It is not necessary to use only negative behaviors in such a code. Often, the counting of positive behaviors, in terms of a positive list of categories, may provide valuable information. Thus, let's assume the negative categories listed above, and also a list of positive categories: Play Nicely (PL); Compliance (CO); Laughing (LA); Volunteering for Work (VW) and Cooperating with Siblings (CS).

The first step is to devise a data collection form as follows:

Name _____
Date _____
Phase _____
Observer _____
Others Present _____
Observation started at _____ a.m./p.m.
Observation ended at _____ a.m./p.m.
TOTAL Minutes Observed _____

NP	C	T	DT	Y	NC	RH
X	X	T		X	X	
X		X		X	X	
X		X			X	
X						
X						
X						
6	1	3		2	3	

Total Negative — 15
Rate/Min.   .5 (15/30)

PL	CO	LA	VW	CS
X	X	X		X
X		X		X
X				
3	1	2		2

Total Positive   8
Rate/Min   .27 (8/30)

As can be seen in the above example, the observer watched the child for 30 minutes. Each time a child behaved in a way codeable in one of the categories, a check was placed in the appropriate column. It is possible to simply add up the columns to get a frequency of each behavior during the observation session. **It is also possible to add up the frequencies and get total negative behaviors and total positive behaviors.** The rate of any behavior is calculated by dividing the total behaviors in any category (or group of categories) by the number of minutes observed.

If it is possible to make all observation sessions of exactly the same duration (e.g., 30 minutes) then one does not have to worry about calculating rates. However, sometimes a child or adult will leave the room for a while, or the observation may be otherwise disrupted, then the time will vary from session to session. In this case, it is absolutely necessary to calculate the *rates* at which the behaviors occur, otherwise it will be impossible to compare the behavior observed from one session to another.

In our own work we have found that the absolute minimum number of half-hour sessions required for any sort of stability is two per phase. We try to get five or six in our work. As will be shown later, it is possible to determine from the data just how many observational sessions will be sufficient to insure reasonably stable data.

Example 2. Suppose that one is interested in measuring aggressive behavior of the same sort described in Example 1 except that one is not interested in the specific kinds of aggressive or prosocial behavior the child emits, only in the total rates of aggressive or prosocial behavior. This would be similar to the Total Deviant Behavior rates described in previous chapters. If one simply needs such an overall estimate, then combine all of the discrete category definitions into one (e.g., Total Aggressive Behavior). In terms of Example 1, one would have two categories on the top of the sheet: Total Aggressive Behavior (TAB), and Total Prosocial Behavior (TPB). One would then have a total of 15 checks in the TAB and 8 checks in the TPB columns. The rates per minute would be the same.

This second approach is quite a bit easier than the first. It is easier to become proficient and it is easier to maintain acceptable data quality. The main problem with the critical incident system is maintaining observer vigilance.

Once the system is pilot tested so that two observers can produce similar data while watching the same subject at the same time, one further step is necessary. The category definitions must be continuously embellished as necessary. For example, one will probably have to decide how to judge when one aggressive behavior ends and another begins, or the difference between play and roughhousing. These decision rules must be written down and should be put together in an observation manual.

Example 3. Suppose one is interested in collecting data on aggressive child behavior as in Example 2. However, one is also interested in the manner in which the parent(s) respond to those behaviors. For example, one may be interested in the following issues: (a) do both parents respond equally to the child when he is behaving in an aggressive manner? (b) do either of the parents do anything when the child is acting appropriately? (c) do the parents react in a consistent manner with the child?

The data form is prepared as in Example 2 with one exception: rows will be made so that the reactions of the parents can be recorded. See Table 5.

TABLE 5

Name _____   Others Present _____

Date _____   Observation started at _____ a.m./p.m.

Phase _____   Observation ended at _____ a.m./p.m.

Observer _____

Child Behavior

	Total Agressive Behavior (TAB)	Total Prosocial Behavior (TPB)	Independent Play (IP)	TOTALS
Mother	+ + - + + +	+ + + (+)* + + + - - + + +	(+) * +	16+ 3-
Father	- - + -	+ + - (+)* + - + +	- (+) *	7+ 6-
No Reaction		//////		6
Totals	10	25*	3*	

* If both parents respond to the same child behavior, put parentheses around the reactions of both parents to that behavior. To calculate total behavior for a category, add all symbols without parentheses to ½ the symbols in parentheses.

Looking at Table 5, each mark entered in any of the three columns indicated that one behavior occurred (note that we have added a third category — independent play — which may be of interest to some). The location in the column of the mark indicated who, if anyone, responded to the behavior. Thus, for Aggressive behaviors, the child was observed to emit 10 aggressive behaviors, four of which were responded to by father, and six by mother (each aggressive child response was reacted to by at least one of the parents). Mother tended to react positively to aggressive child behaviors (5/6 times) and father tended to react negatively (3/4) times. As can be seen in Table 5, it is possible to derive many scores using this sort of format. If one wishes to use such an observational system before and after treatment, it is possible to assess change along a variety of dimensions (e.g., rates of child aggressive, prosocial and independent play behaviors; percent of each class of behaviors consequated by parents; differential rates of positive and negative reactions by parents).

Using this format, a rich variety of data may be obtained without placing undue demands on observers. Repeating a final word of caution: one should decide which data are useful and choose the simplest possible format.

Psychometric Characteristics

As pointed out earlier in this chapter, the value of an observational system is totally dependent upon its psychometric characteristics. In order to have any confidence in the quality of observational data, two questions must be answered: Are the data reliable? Are the data valid? Although related, these questions will be dealt with one at a time.

Reliability refers to the consistency of the data produced by a coding system when different observers use it simultaneously or when the system is used repeatedly during the same assessment phase (an elastic ruler would be unreliable, sometimes it would measure a dollar bill as five inches long, and at other times as seven or eight inches. It would be better to throw such a ruler away and guess at lengths). In the context of observational data, two specific reliability measures are important: interobserver reliability and stability.

Interobserver reliability is the level at which the same data are produced by two observers who make independent, but simultaneous, observations of the same subjects. There are two simple ways to calculate interobserver reliability for critical incident systems: percent agreement and correlation. Correlational procedures, though more elegant, require some sophistication in statistics and will not be dealt with here.

Percent agreement is calculated by taking the protocols (completed coding sheets) from two observers who have independently watched the same subjects and comparing the frequencies of all categories recorded by both observers. Suppose that observer 'A' recorded 15 aggressive behaviors by a given subject. Observer 'B' recorded 20 aggressive behaviors by the same subject during the same period. Simply put the smaller number over the larger (i.e., 15/20) and divide. In this example the interobserver reliability for this session (for the aggressive behavior category) is 75%. To achieve a good estimate of reliability, repeat this procedure for several observations and take the average of the percent agreement scores. For critical incident systems such as described here, the percent agreement scores should average about 80% or higher.

Stability, as used here, is an estimate of the degree to which the behavior ratings, taken on the same subjects, are similar across two or more points in time. Obviously, stability can be affected by the level of interobserver reliability and the magnitude of behavioral differences across time points. Stability can be calculated in a manner similar to that used for observer reliability. Suppose that baseline data are collected on subjects for four consecutive daily observational sessions. The data from the first two sessions should be compared to the data from the last two sessions (if session lengths vary, then rate per minute should be used). Proceed as in calculating observer agreement. If fifteen hits were observed in the first two sessions and twenty hits were observed during the last two sessions, then the stability would be 15/20 or 75%. When this procedure is repeated for several subjects, a picture of the stability of a given code category can be established. If the stability scores are consistently low (e.g. lower than 50%) then you may wish to increase the number of observational sessions for each phase of the study.

Validity is the degree to which the observational scores measure what one thinks they measure. There are two straightforward ways to measure the validity of observational data: comparison of data from known groups of subjects, and correlation of scores with an external criterion measure. As with reliability, the correlational approach is too complex to be dealt with in this chapter.

Comparison of data from known groups is straightforward in concept. One simply compares scores taken from groups of subjects who are known to differ on the measure of interest. To illustrate this approach, suppose that we have two groups of clients: withdrawn and hyperactive children. If our code which is designed to measure aggressiveness is valid, we should expect that, on the average, withdrawn children will have lower scores than hyperactive children. In this example, we might do observations on 15 withdrawn and 15 hyperactive children. Rates per minute would be calculated for each child and analyzed as follows:

hyperactive children		*withdrawn children*	
\multicolumn{4}{c}{*Rates per minute of aggressive behaviors*}			
1	.3	1	.1
2	.4	2	.2
3	.7	3	.5
4	.8	4	.3
5	.2	5	.7
6	.9	6	.2
7	.6	7	.1
8	.8	8	.2
9	.4	9	.1
10	.7	10	.4
11	.3	11	.1
12	.8	12	.2
13	.9	13	.7
14	.5	14	.4
15	.6	15	.3
SUM = 8.90		SUM = 4.50	
$\bar{X}$ = 8.90/15 = .593		$\bar{X}$ = 4.50/15 = .300	

As can be seen in this example, the hyperactive children do, in fact, score much higher than the withdrawn children. Such a finding lends substantial validity to the observational code. The procedure would be the same for testing the validity of any set of categories: find known groups who should be expected to differ on a category if it is valid; observe the groups and compare the scores. In order to be sure that the observed group differences are not achieved by chance, a "t" test can be performed on the data (see any elementary statistics text for the procedure).

As a final note, validity is a moot issue until reliability is established. In other words, one should not proceed to validity analyses until acceptable reliability has been achieved. Finally, the measurement of interobserver reliability is not a one-time thing. At least 10% of all observation data should be taken by two observers and evaluated for reliability.

Summary

The procedures suggested in this chapter require a good deal of careful consideration about the behavior to be measured, and the purpose for the measurement. One should go slowly in developing and checking a new system. After the observation system is acceptable in terms of its face validity, and the cost in producing data, it is absolutely essential to go on to evaluations of reliability and validity described in this chapter. Observational systems which are not repeatedly monitored for reliability and validity provide no better data than does casual observation.

References

Antonovsky, H.F. A contribution to research in the area of mother/child relationships. *Child Development*, 1959, *30*, 37–51.

Arnold, J., Levine, A., & Patterson, G.R. Changes in sibling behavior following family intervention. *Journal of Consulting and Clinical Psychology*, 1975, *43*, 683–688.

Azrin, N., Holtz, W., Ulrich, R., & Goldiamond, I. The control of conversation through reinforcement. *Journal of Experimental Analysis of Behavior*, 1961, *4*, 25–30.

Bales, R.F. *Interaction process analysis.* Cambridge, Mass.: Addison Wesley, 1950.

Barker, R.G. *One boy's day.* New York: Harper and Row, 1951.

Barker, R.G. *Ecological psychology.* Stanford, California: Stanford University Press, 1968.

Barker, R.G., & Wright, H.F. *Midwest and its children.* Evanston, Illinois: Row Peterson, 1954.

Baumrind, D., & Black, H. Socialization practices associated with dimensions of competence in preschool boys and girls. *Child Development*, 1967, *38*, 291–307.

Becker, W. The relationship of factors in parental ratings of self and each other to the behavior of kindergarten children as rated by mothers, fathers, and teachers. *Journal of Consulting Psychology*, 1960, *24*, 507–527.

Bernal, M.E., Gibson, D.M. Williams, D.E., & Pesses, D.I. A device for recording automatic audio tape recording. *Journal of Applied Behavior Analysis*, 1971, *4*, 151–156.

Bing, E. Effect of child-rearing practices on development of differential cognitive abilities. *Child Development*, 1963, *34*, 631–648.

Bobbitt, R., Gourevitch, V., Miller, L., & Jensen, G. Dynamics of social interaction behavior: A computerized procedure for analyzing trends, patterns, and sequences. *Psychological Bulletin*, 1969, *71*, 110–112.

Buehler, R.E., Patterson, G.R., & Furniss, J.M. The reinforcement of behavior in institutional settings. *Behaviour Research and Therapy.* 1966, *4*, 157–167.

Burton, R.V. Validity of retrospective reports assessed by the multi-trait, multi-method analyses. Developmental Psychology Monograph, 1970, *3*, (3).

Caldwell, B.M. A new "approach" to behavioral ecology. In J.P. Hill (Ed.), *Minnesota Symposia on Child Psychology.* Vol. 2. Minneapolis: University of Minnesota Press, 1969.

Caldwell, B.M. A new approach to behavioral Ecology. In J.P. Hill (Ed.), *Minnesota Symposia on Child Psychology.* Vol. 5. Minneapolis: University of Minnesota Press, 1971.

Candland, D.K., Dresdale, L., Leiphart, J.C., & Johnson, M. Videotape as a replacement for the human observer in studies of non-human primate behavior. *Behavior Research Methods and Instrumentation*, 1972, *4*, 24–26.

Christensen, A. Cost effectiveness in behavior family therapy. Unpublished Ph.D. dissertation, University of Oregon, 1976.

Clement, P.W., & Milne, D.C. Group play therapy and tangible reinforcers used to modify the behavior of eight-year-old boys. *Behaviour Research and Therapy*, 1967, *5*, 301–312.

Cohen, J.A. Coefficient of agreement for nominal scales. *Educational and Psychological Measurement*, 1960, *20*, (1), 37–46.

Collins, R.C. The treatment of disruptive behavior problems by employment of a partial-milieu consistency program. Unpublished doctoral dissertation, University of Oregon, 1966.

Connolly, K., & Smith, P.K. Reactions of preschool children to a strange observer. In N. Blurton–Jones (Ed.), *Ethological studies of child behavior.* Cambridge: Cambridge University Press, 1972.

Cronback, L.J., Gleser, G.C., Nanda, H., & Rajaratnam, N. *The dependability of behavioral measurements: Theory of generalizability for scores and profiles.* New York: John Wiley & Sons, 1972.

DeMaster, B., Reid, J.B., & Twentyman, C. The effects of different amounts of feedback on observers' reliability. *Behavior Therapy*, 1976, in press.

Douglas, J.W., Lawson, A., Cooper, J.E. & Cooper, E. Family interaction and the activities of young children. *Journal of Child Psychology and Psychiatry*, 1968, *9*, 157–171.

Fleischman, M.J. The effects of parenting salary and family SES in the social learning treatment of aggressive children. Unpublished Ph.D. dissertation, University of Oregon, 1976.

Goodenough, F.L. Inter-relationships in the behavior of young children. *Child Development*, 1930, *1*, 29–47.

Graziano, A.M., & Fink, R.S. Second-order effects in mental health treatments. *Journal of Consulting and Clinical Psychology*, 1973, *40*, 356–364.

Grimm, J.A., Parsons, J.A., & Bijou, S.W. A technique for minimizing subject-observer looking interactions in a field setting. *Journal of Experimental Child Psychology*, 1972, *14*, 500–505.

Gulliksen, H. *Theory of mental tests*. New York: John Wiley & Sons, 1950.

Harris, A.M. Observer effect on family interaction. Unpublished doctoral dissertation, University of Oregon, 1969.

Herbert, E. Parent programs — bringing it all back home. Paper presented at the meeting of the American Psychological Association, Miami, 1970.

Heyns, R.W. & Lippitt, R. Systematic observational techniques. In G. Lindzey (Ed.), *Handbook of social psychology*. Vol. 1. Cambridge, Massachusetts: Addison–Wesley, 1954.

Honig, A.S., Tannenbaum, J., & Caldwell, B. Maternal behavior in verbal report and in laboratory observations. Paper presented at the meeting of the American Psychological Association, San Francisco, 1968.

Hunt, J. *Intelligence and experience*. New York: Ronald Press, 1961.

Johnson, S.M. & Bolstad, O.D. Methodological issues in naturalistic observations: Some problems and solutions for field research. In L.A. Hamerlynck, L.C. Handy, & E.J. Mash (Eds.), *Behavior change: Methodology concepts and practice*. Champaign, Illinois: Research Press, 1973. Pp. 7–68.

Johnson, S.M., & Bolstad, O.D. Reactivity to home observation: A comparison of audio and recorded behavior with observers present or absent. Unpublished manuscript, University of Oregon, 1974.

Johnson, S.M., & Lobitz, G.K. Parental manipulations of child behavior in home observations. *Journal of Applied Behavior Analysis*, 1974, *7*, 23–31.

Johnson, S.M., & Christensen, A. Multiple criteria follow-up of behavior modification with families. *Journal of Abnormal Child Psycholgy*, 1975, *3*, 135–154.

Jones, R.R. Behavioral observation and frequency data: Problems in scoring, analysis, and interpretation. In L.A. Hamerlynck, L.C. Handy, & E.J. Mash (Eds.), *Behavior change: Methodology concepts and practice*. Champaign, Illinois: Research Press, 1973.

Jones, R.R., Reid, J.B., & Patterson, G.R. Naturalistic observations in clinical assessment. In P. McReynolds (Ed.), *Advances in psychological assessment*. Vol. 3. San Francisco: Jossey-Bass, 1975. Pp. 42–95.

Kent, R.N., O'Leary, K.D., Diament, C., & Dietz, A. Expectation biases in observational evaluation of therapeutic change. *Journal of Abnormal Psychology*, 1974, in press.

Kopfstein, D. The effects of accelerating and decelerating consequences on the social behavior of trainable retarded children. *Child Development*, 1972, *43*, 800–809.

Lapouse, R., & Monk, M.A. An epidemiologic study of behavior characteristics in children. *American Journal of Public Health*, 1958, *48*, 1139–1143.

Levitt, E.E. The results of psychotherapy with children: An evaluation. *Journal of Consulting Psychology*, 1957, *21*, 189–196.

Levitt, E.E. Research on psychotherapy with children: In A. Bergin & S. Garfield (Eds.), *Handbook of psychotherapy and behavior change*. New York: John Wiley & Sons, 1971.

Lobitz, G.K., & Johnson, S.M. Parental manipulation of the behavior of normal and deviant children. *Child Development*, 1976, in press.

Lytten, H. Observation studies of parent-child interaction: A methodological review. *Child Development*, 1971, *42*, 651–684.

Mash, E.J. Behavior modification and methodology: A developmental perspective. *The Journal of Educational Thought*, 1976, *10*, 5–21.

Masling, J., & Stern, G. Effect of the observer in the classroom. *Journal of Educational Psychology*, 1969, *60*, 351–354.

Mcfarlene, J., Allen, L., & Honzik, M. *A developmental study of the behavior problems of normal children between twenty-one months and 14 years*. Berkeley, California: University of California Press, 1962.

Mercatoris, M., & Craighead, W.E. The effect of nonparticipant observation on teacher and pupil classroom behavior. *Journal of Educational Psychology*, 1973, in press.

Moos, R. Behavior effects of being observed: Reactions to a wireless radio transmitter, *Journal of Consulting and Clinical Psychology*, 1968, *32*, 383–388.

Moustakas, C.E., Sigel, I., & Schalock, H. An objective method for the measurement and analysis of child/adult interaction. *Child Development*, 1956, *27*, 109–134.

Novick, J., Rosenfeld, E., & Block, D. Situational variations in the behavior of children. Paper presented at the Social Research for Child Development Conference, Minneapolis, Minnesota, 1965.

O'Conner, R. Relative efficacy of modelling, shaping, and the combined procedures for modification of socially withdrawn children. *Journal of Abnormal Psychology*, 1972, *79*, 327–334.

O'Leary, K.D., Kent, R.N., & Karpowitz, J. Shaping data collection congruent with experimental hypotheses. *Journal of Applied Behavior Analysis*, 1975, *8*, 43–51.

Olson, W. The incidence of nervous habits in children. *Journal of Abnormal Social Psychology*, 1930, *35*, 75–92.

Patterson, G.R. Interventions for boys with conduct problems: Multiple settings, treatments, and criteria. *Journal of Consulting and Clinical Psychology*, 1974, *42*, 471–481. (a)

Patterson, G.R. Retraining of aggressive boys by their parents: Review of recent literature and follow-up evaluation. *Canadian Psychiatric Association Journal*, 1974, *19*, 142–161. (b)

Patterson, G.R. A basis for identifying stimuli which control behaviors in natural settings. *Child Development*, 1974, *45*, 900–911. (c)

Patterson, G.R. Multiple evaluations of a parent training program. In T. Thompson & W.S. Dockens III (Eds.), *Applications of behavior modification*. New York: Academic Press, 1975, 299–322.

Patterson, G.R. The aggressive child: Victim and architect of a coercive system. In E.J. Mash, L.A. Hamerlynck, & L.C. Handy (Eds.), *Behavior modification and families*.

Patterson, G.R., & Cobb, J.A. A dyadic analysis of "aggressive" behaviors. In J.P. Hill (Ed.), *Minnesota Symposia on Child Psychology*. Vol. 5. Minneapolis: University of Minnesota, 1971. Pp. 72–129.

Patterson, G.R., & Cobb, J.A. Stimulus control for classes of noxious behaviors. In J.F. Knutson (Ed.), *The control of aggression: Implications from basic research*. Chicago: Aldine, 1973. Pp. 144–199. See NAPS Document #02107 for 13 pages of supplementary material. Order from ASIS/NAPS, c/o Microfiche Publications, 440 Park Avenue South, New York, N.Y. 10016. Remit in advance $1.50 for microfiche or $5.00 for photocopies up to 30 pages. Make checks payable to Microfiche Publications.

Patterson, G.R., Cobb, J.A., & Ray, R.S. A social engineering technology for retraining the families of aggressive boys. In H.E. Adams & I.P. Unikel (Eds.) *Issues and trends in behavior therapy*. Springfield, Illinois: C.C. Thomas, 1973. Pp. 139–224.

Patterson, G.R., McNeal, S.A., Hawkins, N., & Phelps, R. Reprogramming the social environment. *Journal of Child Psychology and Psychiatry*, 1967, *8*, 181–195.

Patterson, G.R., Ray, R.S., & Shaw, D.A. Direct intervention in families of deviant children. *Oregon Research Institute Research Bulletin*, 1968, *8*, No. 9.

Patterson, G.R., Ray, R.S., Shaw, D.A., & Cobb, J.A. Manual for coding of family interactions, 1969 revision. See NAPS Document #01234 for 33 pages of material. Order from ASIS/NAPS, c/o Microfiche Publications, 440 Park Avenue South, New York, New York 10016. Remit in advance $5.45 for photocopies, $1.50 for microfiche. Make checks payable to Microfiche Publications.

Patterson, G.R., & Reid, J.B. Reciprocity and coercion: Two facets of social systems. In C. Neuringer & J.L. Michael (Eds.), *Behavior modification in clinical psychology*. New York: Appleton-Century Crofts, 1970. Pp. 133–177.

Patterson G.R., & Reid, J.B. Intervention for families of aggressive boys: A replication study. *Behaviour Research and Therapy*, 1973, *11*, 383–394.

Patterson, G.R., Reid, J.B., Jones, R.R., & Conger, R.E. *A social learning approach to family intervention. Vol. 1. Families with aggressive children*. Eugene, Oregon: Castalia Publishing Company, 1975.

Paul, J.S. Observer influence on the interactive behavior of a mother and a single child in the home. Unpublished master's thesis, Oregon State University, 1963.

Peine, H. Behavioral recording by parents and its resultant consequences. Unpublished master's thesis, University of Utah, 1970.

Purcell, K., & Brady, K. Adaptation to the invasion of privacy: Monitoring behavior with a miniature radio transmitter. *Merrill Palmer Quarterly of Behavior and Development*, 1966, *12*, 242–254.

Rausch, H.L. Interaction sequences. *Journal of Personality and Social Psychology*, 1965, *2*, 487–499.

Reid, J.B. Reliability assessment of observation data: A possible methodological problem. *Child Development*, 1970, *41*, 1143–1150.

Reid, J.B., & Hendriks, A.F.C.J. A preliminary analysis of the effectiveness of direct home intervention for treatment of predelinquent boys who steal. In L.A. Hamerlynck, L.C. Handy, & E.J. Mash (Eds.), *Behavior therapy: Methodology concepts and practice*. Champaign, Illinois: Research Press, 1973.

Reid, J.B., & Hinojosa, G. Evaluation of a program for children who steal. Submitted for publication, 1977.

Reid, J.B., & Patterson, G.R. The modification of aggression and stealing behavior of boys in the home setting. In A. Bandura & E. Ribes (Eds.), *Behavior modification: Experimental analyses of aggression and delinquency*. Hillsdale, New Jersey: Lawrence Erlbaum Associates, 1976. Pp. 123–145.

Reid, J.B., Skindrud, K.D., Taplin, P.S., & Jones, R.R. The role of complexity in the collection and evaluation of observation data. Paper presented at the meeting of the American Psychological Association, Montreal, Quebec, Canada, August 1973.

Robins, L.C. The accuracy of parental recall of aspects of child development and child-rearing practices. *Journal of Abnormal Social Psychology*, 1963, *66*, 261–270.

Romanczyk, R.G., Kent, R.N., Diament, C., & O'Leary, K.D. Methodological problems in naturalistic observation. Paper presented at the Second Annual Symposium on Behavior Analysis, Lawrence, Kansas, May 1971.

Rosenthal, R. *Experimenter effects in behavioral research*. New York: Appleton-Century-Crofts, 1966.

Rosenthal, R., & Fode, K.L. Three experiments in experimenter bias. *Psychological Reports*, 1963, *12*, 491–511.

Rosenthal, R., & Lawson, R. A longitudinal study of the effects of experimenter bias on the operant learning of laboratory rats. *Journal of Psychiatric Research*, 1964, *2*, 61–72.

Rutter, M., Tyzard, J., & Whitmore, R. *Education, health, and behavior*. New York: John Wiley & Sons, 1970.

Schelle, J. A brief report on invalidity of parent evaluations of behavior change. *Journal of Applied Behavior Analysis*, 1974, *7*, 341–343.

Schoggin, P. Mechanical aids for making specimen records of behavior. *Child Development*, 1964, *35*, 985–989.

Sears, R.R. Comparison of interviews with questionnaires for measuring mother attitudes toward sex and aggression. *Journal of Personality and Social Psychology*, 1965, *2*, 37–44.

Skindrud, K.D. An evaluation of observer bias in experimental field studies of social interaction. Unpublished doctoral dissertation, University of Oregon, 1972.

Smith, H.T. A comparison of interview and observation measures of mother behavior. *Journal of Abnormal and Social Psychology*, 1958, *57*, 278–287.

Surrott, P.R., Ulrich, R.E., & Hawkins, R.P. An elementary student as a behavioral engineer. *Journal of Applied Behavior Analysis*, 1969, *2*, 85–92.

Taplin, P.S. Changes in parental consequation as a function of intervention. Unpublished doctoral dissertation, University of Wisconsin, 1974.

Taplin, P.S., & Reid, J.B. Effects of instructional set and experimental influence on observer reliability. *Child Development*, 1973, *44*, 547–554.

Taplin, P.S., & Reid, J.B. Changes in parental consequation as a function of family intervention. *Journal of Consulting and Clinical Psychology*, 1976, in press.

Thomas, D.R., Becker, W.C., & Armstrong, M. Production and elimination of disruptive classroom behavior by systematically varying teacher's behavior. *Journal of Applied Behavior Analysis*, 1968, *1*, 34–45.

Thomas, D., Loomis, A., & Arrington, R. *Observational studies of social behavior. Vol. 1.*

Social behavior patterns. New Haven, Connecticut: Yale University Press, 1933.

Waksman, S. An empirical investigation of Campbell and Fiske's multistate-multimetrics using social learning measures. *Journal of Abnormal Child Psychology,* 1977, in press.

Walter, H.I., & Gilmore, S.K. Placebo versus social learning effects in parent training procedures designed to alter the behaviors of aggressive boys. *Behavior Therapy,* 1973, *4,* 361–377.

Weick, K.E. Systematic observational methods. In G. Lindzey & A. Aronson (Eds.), *The handbook of social psychology.* Vol. 2, 2nd Edition. Reeding, Mass.: Addison Wesley, 1968.

White, G.D. The effects of observer presence on family behaviors. Unpublished doctoral dissertation, University of Oregon, 1972.

Wiggins, J.S. Observation techniques: I. Generalizability and facets of observation. In *Personality and prediction: Principles of personality assessment.* Reeding, Massachusetts: Addison-Wesley, 1973. (a)

Wiggins, J.S. *Personality and prediction: Principles of personality assessment.* Reeding, Massachusetts: Addison-Wesley, 1973. (b)

Willems, E.P., & Raush, H.L. *Naturalistic viewpoints in psychological research.* New York: Holt, Rinehart & Winston, 1969.

Wiltz, N.A., & Patterson, G.R. An evaluation of parent training procedures designed to alter inappropriate aggressive behavior of boys. *Behavior Therapy,* 1974, *5,* 215–221.

Wright, H.F. Observational child study. In P. Mussen (Ed.), *Handbook of research methods in child development.* New York: John Wiley & Sons, 1960.

Yarrow, M.R., Campbell, J., & Burton, R.V. Reliability of maternal retrospection: A preliminary report. *Family Process,* 1964, *3,* 207–218.

Yarrow, M.R., Campbell, J., & Burton, R.V. Recollections of childhood: A study of the retrospective method. *Monographs of the Society for Research in Child Development,* 1970, *35,* Serial No. 138.

Yarrow, M.R., & Waxler, C.Z. Observing interaction: A confrontation with methodology. In R. Cairns (Ed.), *Social interaction: Methods, analyses, and illustrations.* Chicago: University of Chicago Press, 1976.

Zergiob, L., Arnold, S., & Forehand, R. An examination of observer effects in parent/child interaction. *Child Development,* 1975, *46,* 509–512.

Appendices

Appendix 1
Sample Observer Coding Sheet

Appendix 2
Schematic: Behavior Observation Timer

Appendix 3
Identified Boys:
Behavior Rates During Baseline

Appendix 4
Girls in Family:
Behavior Rates During Baseline

Appendix 5
Sibling by Sex:
Behavior Rates During Baseline

Appendix 6
All Siblings:
Behavior Rates During Baseline

Appendix 7
All Children in Family:
Behavior Rates During Baseline

Appendix 8
Parents:
Behavior Rates During Baseline

Appendix 9
All Family Members:
Behavior Rates During Baseline

Appendix 10
Demographic Information on Stealers, Non-Stealers, and Normals in Present Sample

Appendix 11
Z Scores of Total Deviant Behavior Category for Deviant Child Sample at Baseline, Termination, and Follow-up

Appendix 12
Z Score Transformation Table for Coercive Behavior Rates

Appendix 13
Observer Reliability: Percent Agreement and Correlation

APPENDIX ONE
SAMPLE OBSERVER CODING SHEET

BEHAVIOR RATING SHEET

ID Number

Sheet No.

Subject _____ Observer _____ Date _____

APPENDIX TWO

SCHEMATIC: BEHAVIOR OBSERVATION TIMER

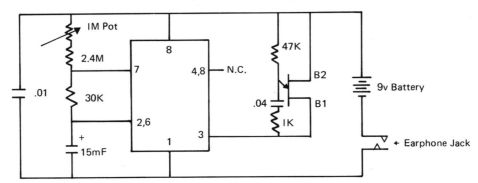

I.C. is 555 type timer
Transister is Unijunction type (Motorola HEP 310 is suitable)

Preassembled timers or kits of a circuit similar to the above are available from:
RCS Enterprises
2287 Olive St.
Eugene, OR 97405

The general approach taken in developing the Family Interaction Coding System was to view it simply as an instrument for collecting data. Its psychometric properties were reviewed in chapter 3. In that context we thought it would be useful to other investigators to provide extensive normative data by age, sex, and status as either normal or deviant. The samples available at the time of this writing hardly warrant the term "normative sample"; such data are currently being collected. The available data are summarized here in Appendices three through ten. Appendices eleven and twelve provide Z scores of total deviant behavior for a deviant child sample and a Z score transformation table for coercive behavior rates. Appendix thirteen provides observer reliability data for eleven protocols.

APPENDIX THREE

IDENTIFIED BOYS: BEHAVIOR RATES DURING BASELINE

Behavior		Identified deviants (N=27 families) (N=27 subjects)	Boys (6 years or under) (N=9 families) N=10 subjects)	Boys (7 years or over) (N=23 families) (N=37 subjects)	Matched normals (N=27 families) (N=27 subjects)	Normals (6 years or under) (N=11 families) (N=15 subjects)	Normals (7 years or over) (N=23 families) (N=37 subjects)
Total Social Behavior	$\bar{x}$	6.829	6.313	7.023	5.930	6.094	5.748
	SD	1.904	1.663	1.881	1.698	1.176	1.564
Total Deviant Behavior	$\bar{x}$	0.661	0.699	0.604	0.277	0.581	0.221
	SD	0.641	0.573	0.601	0.359	0.543	0.149
Approval	$\bar{x}$	0.017	0.031	0.011	0.028	0.031	0.030
	SD	0.024	0.032	0.018	0.022	0.023	0.021
Attention	$\bar{x}$	1.382	1.409	1.293	1.387	1.542	1.211
	SD	0.645	0.491	0.509	0.632	0.567	0.509
Command	$\bar{x}$	0.048	0.042	0.063	0.039	0.043	0.040
	SD	0.051	0.026	0.061	0.038	0.036	0.036
Command Negative*	$\bar{x}$	0.008	0.006	0.007	0.002	0.005	0.003
	SD	0.015	0.017	0.012	0.005	0.007	0.006
Compliance	$\bar{x}$	0.226	0.372	0.171	0.181	0.217	0.178
	SD	0.170	0.153	0.125	0.119	0.145	0.127
Cry*	$\bar{x}$	0.019	0.009	0.021	0.002	0.016	0.000
	SD	0.059	0.017	0.062	0.012	0.024	0.000
Disapproval*	$\bar{x}$	0.134	0.115	0.141	0.084	0.111	0.083
	SD	0.109	0.136	0.093	0.067	0.088	0.054
Dependency*	$\bar{x}$	0.007	0.004	0.008	0.003	0.006	0.003
	SD	0.022	0.013	0.023	0.008	0.009	0.008
Destructiveness*	$\bar{x}$	0.031	0.017	0.035	0.006	0.009	0.003
	SD	0.079	0.039	0.083	0.012	0.013	0.008
High Rate*	$\bar{x}$	0.044	0.064	0.055	0.014	0.042	0.012
	SD	0.136	0.176	0.147	0.040	0.063	0.027
Humiliate*	$\bar{x}$	0.020	0.012	0.022	0.001	0.004	0.002
	SD	0.035	0.015	0.031	0.004	0.007	0.005
Ignore*	$\bar{x}$	0.005	0.002	0.007	0.004	0.004	0.002
	SD	0.009	0.006	0.010	0.009	0.008	0.005
Indulgence	$\bar{x}$	0.000	0.000	0.000	0.000	0.000	0.000
	SD	0.000	0.000	0.000	0.000	0.000	0.000
Laugh	$\bar{x}$	0.081	0.099	0.089	0.110	0.187	0.130
	SD	0.068	0.087	0.059	0.110	0.241	0.115
Non-Compliance*	$\bar{x}$	0.092	0.140	0.064	0.050	0.088	0.044
	SD	0.093	0.108	0.058	0.055	0.070	0.051
Negativism*	$\bar{x}$	0.115	0.114	0.091	0.025	0.013	0.024
	SD	0.156	0.151	0.120	0.030	0.030	0.024
Normative	$\bar{x}$	2.703	2.351	2.793	2.562	2.160	2.660
	SD	1.081	0.809	0.892	1.155	0.801	1.156
No Response	$\bar{x}$	0.071	0.072	0.078	0.055	0.055	0.061
	SD	0.052	0.034	0.071	0.043	0.028	0.044
Play	$\bar{x}$	2.006	2.455	1.983	2.502	2.951	2.498
	SD	1.370	1.242	1.286	1.697	1.614	1.687

* Denotes catagories of behavior classed as aversive.
1 Catagory includes identified deviant males in age group plus male siblings in same age group.

APPENDIX THREE CONTINUED

Behavior		Identified deviants (N=27 families) (N=27 subjects)	Boys (6 years or under) 1 (N=9 families) (N=10 subjects)	Boys (7 years or over) 1 (N=23 families) (N=37 subjects)	Matched normals (N=27 families) (N=27 subjects)	Boys (6 years or under) (N=11 families) (N=15 subjects)	Boys (7 years or over) 1 (N=23 families) (N=37 subjects)
Physical Negative*	$\bar{x}$	0.042	0.032	0.041	0.009	0.029	0.009
	SD	0.063	0.038	0.059	0.022	0.027	0.016
Physical Positive	$\bar{x}$	0.039	0.097	0.040	0.014	0.044	0.009
	SD	0.090	0.137	0.095	0.039	0.060	0.016
Proximity	$\bar{x}$	0.014	0.044	0.019	0.003	0.006	0.001
	SD	0.038	0.116	0.041	0.014	0.021	0.002
Receive	$\bar{x}$	0.054	0.102	0.045	0.031	0.111	0.022
	SD	0.083	0.100	0.079	0.040	0.073	0.029
Self-Stimulation	$\bar{x}$	0.216	0.094	0.220	0.109	0.226	0.082
	SD	0.236	0.105	0.244	0.134	0.305	0.104
Talk	$\bar{x}$	2.238	2.115	2.113	2.027	1.919	1.976
	SD	0.694	0.909	0.556	0.737	0.651	0.715
Tease*	$\bar{x}$	0.050	0.046	0.043	0.020	0.020	0.023
	SD	0.061	0.089	0.040	0.036	0.040	0.039
Touch	$\bar{x}$	0.017	0.039	0.017	0.011	0.005	0.012
	SD	0.026	0.060	0.028	0.017	0.012	0.020
Whine*	$\bar{x}$	0.036	0.083	0.023	0.039	0.124	0.009
	SD	0.055	0.069	0.036	0.116	0.176	0.013
Work	$\bar{x}$	0.622	0.302	0.860	0.971	0.288	1.158
	SD	0.730	0.582	0.787	1.071	0.248	1.125
Yell*	$\bar{x}$	0.057	0.055	0.046	0.018	0.108	0.005
	SD	0.084	0.068	0.082	0.079	0.198	0.010

* Denotes categories of behavior classed as aversive.
1 Category includes identified deviant males In age group plus male siblings in same age group.

APPENDIX FOUR

GIRLS IN FAMILY: BEHAVIOR RATES DURING BASELINE

Behavior		Deviant Families		Normal Families	
		Girls 6 years and under (N=10 families) (N=12 subjects)	Girls 7 years and over (N=17 families) (N=22 subjects)	Girls 6 years and under (N=6 families) (N=7 subjects)	Girls 7 years and over (N=18 families) (N=22 subjects)
Total Social Behavior	$\bar{x}$ SD	7.209 2.462	5.961 2.214	6.469 1.931	5.678 1.435
Total Deviant Behavior	$\bar{x}$ SD	0.666 0.473	0.427 0.490	0.514 0.256	0.215 0.214
Approval	$\bar{x}$ SD	0.010 0.013	0.011 0.013	0.021 0.015	0.031 0.029
Attention	$\bar{x}$ SD	1.786 0.614	1.035 0.568	2.007 0.408	1.154 0.457
Command	$\bar{x}$ SD	0.053 0.023	0.046 0.041	0.022 0.021	0.043 0.028
Command Negative	$\bar{x}$ SD	0.009 0.016	0.014 0.028	0.000 0.000	0.002 0.005
Compliance	$\bar{x}$ SD	0.177 0.065	0.096 0.064	0.249 0.122	0.101 0.082
Cry*	$\bar{x}$ SD	0.080 0.095	0.004 0.011	0.114 0.125	0.018 0.037
Disapproval*	$\bar{x}$ SD	0.090 0.038	0.137 0.143	0.054 0.045	0.083 0.054
Dependency*	$\bar{x}$ SD	0.015 0.037	0.008 0.022	0.008 0.016	0.001 0.002
Destructiveness*	$\bar{x}$ SD	0.016 0.024	0.005 0.016	0.007 0.008	0.001 0.002
High Rate*	$\bar{x}$ SD	0.038 0.077	0.044 0.099	0.020 0.024	0.001 0.003
Humiliate*	$\bar{x}$ SD	0.004 0.008	0.019 0.032	0.000 0.000	0.004 0.009
Ignore*	$\bar{x}$ SD	0.004 0.011	0.012 0.014	0.000 0.000	0.004 0.012
Indulgence	$\bar{x}$ SD	0.001 0.003	0.000 0.000	0.000 0.000	0.000 0.000
Laugh	$\bar{x}$ SD	0.085 0.086	0.129 0.112	0.107 0.051	0.134 0.098
Non Compliance*	$\bar{x}$ SD	0.107 0.079	0.040 0.055	0.078 0.048	0.021 0.033
Negativism*	$\bar{x}$ SD	0.038 0.053	0.060 0.087	0.031 0.032	0.032 0.050
Normative	$\bar{x}$ SD	2.626 0.605	3.244 1.321	2.774 0.638	3.056 0.999
No Response	$\bar{x}$ SD	0.047 0.038	0.049 0.028	0.029 0.018	0.055 0.045
Play	$\bar{x}$ SD	2.392 1.666	2.080 1.821	2.552 0.984	2.330 1.476

* Denotes catagories of behavior classed as aversive.

APPENDIX FOUR CONTINUED

		Deviant Families		Normal Families	
		Girls 6 years and under (N=10 families) (N=12 subjects)	Girls 7 years and over (N=17 families) (N=22 subjects)	Girls 6 years and under (N=6 families) (N=7 subjects)	Girls 7 years and over (N=18 families) (N=22 subjects)
Behavior					
Physical Negative*	$\bar{x}$	0.018	0.020	0.013	0.008
	SD	0.028	0.030	0.013	0.017
Physical Positive	$\bar{x}$	0.018	0.078	0.037	0.026
	SD	0.037	0.210	0.063	0.077
Proximity	$\bar{x}$	0.021	0.022	0.071	0.000
	SD	0.063	0.040	0.171	0.000
Receive	$\bar{x}$	0.118	0.007	0.116	0.019
	SD	0.121	0.010	0.098	0.028
Self-Stimulation	$\bar{x}$	0.358	0.225	0.237	0.074
	SD	0.198	0.308	0.092	0.088
Talk	$\bar{x}$	1.619	1.491	1.431	1.657
	SD	0.643	0.627	0.376	0.587
Tease*	$\bar{x}$	0.033	0.019	0.040	0.005
	SD	0.072	0.037	0.038	0.011
Touch	$\bar{x}$	0.009	0.012	0.078	0.014
	SD	0.015	0.015	0.115	0.024
Whine*	$\bar{x}$	0.118	0.019	0.137	0.026
	SD	0.111	0.021	0.169	0.055
Work	$\bar{x}$	0.362	1.458	0.165	1.380
	SD	0.893	1.125	0.217	1.234
Yell*	$\bar{x}$	0.094	0.026	0.013	0.008
	SD	0.132	0.050	0.015	0.019

* Denotes categories of behavior classed as aversive.

APPENDIX FIVE

SIBLING BY SEX: BEHAVIOR RATES DURING BASELINE

Behavior		Deviant Families		Normal Families	
		Total male sibs N=20	Total female sibs N=34	Total male sibs N=25	Total female sibs N=29
Total Social Behavior	$\bar{x}$ SD	6.705 1.865	6.446 2.335	5.877 1.477	5.789 1.466
Total Deviant Behavior	$\bar{x}$ SD	0.484 0.406	0.509 0.471	0.347 0.269	0.257 0.238
Approval	$\bar{x}$ SD	0.011 0.017	0.010 0.013	0.025 0.018	0.031 0.027
Attention	$\bar{x}$ SD	1.269 0.512	1.340 0.669	1.271 0.488	1.332 0.585
Command	$\bar{x}$ SD	0.059 0.055	0.046 0.029	0.036 0.029	0.037 0.027
Command Negative*	$\bar{x}$ SD	0.005 0.012	0.011 0.024	0.005 0.009	0.001 0.004
Compliance	$\bar{x}$ SD	0.178 0.125	0.117 0.068	0.167 0.149	0.123 0.095
Cry*	$\bar{x}$ SD	0.006 0.014	0.028 0.060	0.008 0.018	0.039 0.079
Disapproval*	$\bar{x}$ SD	0.127 0.099	0.126 0.122	0.086 0.066	0.072 0.041
Dependency*	$\bar{x}$ SD	0.002 0.006	0.012 0.030	0.005 0.012	0.002 0.006
Destructiveness*	$\bar{x}$ SD	0.021 0.064	0.007 0.016	0.004 0.009	0.002 0.004
High Rate*	$\bar{x}$ SD	0.051 0.141	0.044 0.093	0.026 0.049	0.005 0.011
Humiliate*	$\bar{x}$ SD	0.019 0.021	0.014 0.028	0.005 0.009	0.003 0.008
Ignore	$\bar{x}$ SD	0.007 0.015	0.009 0.013	0.003 0.006	0.003 0.006
Indulgence	$\bar{x}$ SD	0.000 0.000	0.000 0.001	0.000 0.000	0.000 0.000
Laugh	$\bar{x}$ SD	0.111 0.074	0.120 0.106	0.176 0.193	0.134 0.090
Non-Compliance*	$\bar{x}$ SD	0.060 0.043	0.062 0.065	0.056 0.062	0.030 0.033
Negativism*	$\bar{x}$ SD	0.078 0.119	0.053 0.080	0.017 0.024	0.026 0.034
Normative	$\bar{x}$ SD	3.017 0.747	3.076 1.165	2.849 1.276	2.975 0.960
No Response	$\bar{x}$ SD	0.099 0.107	0.050 0.031	0.067 0.050	0.052 0.042
Play	$\bar{x}$ SD	1.835 1.409	2.090 1.655	2.726 1.706	2.318 1.369

* Denotes categories of behavior classed as aversive.

APPENDIX FIVE CONTINUED

SIBLING BY SEX: BEHAVIOR RATES DURING BASELINE

Behavior		Deviant Families		Normal Families	
		Total male sibs N=20	Total female sibs N=34	Total male sibs N=25	Total female sibs N=29
Physical Negative*	$\bar{x}$	0.029	0.019	0.020	0.008
	SD	0.033	0.027	0.021	0.013
Physical Positive	$\bar{x}$	0.043	0.055	0.029	0.032
	SD	0.058	0.176	0.047	0.077
Proximity	$\bar{x}$	0.033	0.022	0.000	0.010
	SD	0.090	0.042	0.000	0.046
Receive	$\bar{x}$	0.037	0.044	0.069	0.039
	SD	0.047	0.081	0.086	0.054
Self-Stimulation	$\bar{x}$	0.114	0.291	0.124	0.105
	SD	0.144	0.278	0.243	0.111
Talk	$\bar{x}$	1.911	1.600	1.671	1.644
	SD	0.641	0.615	0.601	0.565
Tease*	$\bar{x}$	0.033	0.027	0.021	0.014
	SD	0.041	0.055	0.033	0.026
Touch	$\bar{x}$	0.020	0.011	0.012	0.023
	SD	0.041	0.015	0.024	0.044
Whine*	$\bar{x}$	0.032	0.052	0.044	0.046
	SD	0.059	0.075	0.066	0.081
Work	$\bar{x}$	1.037	1.011	0.664	1.201
	SD	0.976	0.935	0.742	1.225
Yell*	$\bar{x}$	0.014	0.043	0.049	0.007
	SD	0.023	0.058	0.136	0.015

* Denotes categories of behavior classed as aversive.

APPENDIX SIX

ALL SIBLINGS: BEHAVIOR RATES DURING BASELINE

Behavior		Deviant Families All siblings (N=26 families) (N=54 siblings)	Normal Families All siblings (N=27 families) (N=54 siblings)	Behavior		Deviant Families All siblings (N=26 families) (N=54 siblings)	Normal Families All siblings (N=27 families) (N=54 siblings)
Total Social Behavior	$\bar{x}$ SD	6.517 2.152	5.76 1.34	Non-Compliance*	$\bar{x}$ SD	0.064 0.052	0.050 0.055
Total Deviant Behavior	$\bar{x}$ SD	0.499 0.416	0.332 0.256	Negativism*	$\bar{x}$ SD	0.059 0.082	0.023 0.031
Approval	$\bar{x}$ SD	0.011 0.011	0.028 0.019	Normative	$\bar{x}$ SD	3.049 0.899	2.835 0.986
Attention	$\bar{x}$ SD	1.374 0.586	1.385 0.559	No Response	$\bar{x}$ SD	0.074 0.077	0.057 0.040
Command	$\bar{x}$ SD	0.050 0.032	0.036 0.024	Play	$\bar{x}$ SD	1.973 1.519	2.417 1.330
Command Negative*	$\bar{x}$ SD	0.008 0.014	0.003 0.005	Physical Negative*	$\bar{x}$ SD	0.021 0.026	0.014 0.015
Compliance	$\bar{x}$ SD	0.146 0.100	0.168 0.131	Physical Positive	$\bar{x}$ SD	0.063 0.170	0.034 0.054
Cry*	$\bar{x}$ SD	0.024 0.055	0.031 0.067	Proximity	$\bar{x}$ SD	0.023 0.052	0.008 0.040
Disapproval*	$\bar{x}$ SD	0.120 0.095	0.083 0.056	Receive	$\bar{x}$ SD	0.047 0.078	0.065 0.078
Dependency*	$\bar{x}$ SD	0.008 0.024	0.004 0.011	Self-Stimulation	$\bar{x}$ SD	0.223 0.190	0.135 0.206
Destructiveness*	$\bar{x}$ SD	0.011 0.029	0.002 0.005	Talk	$\bar{x}$ SD	1.731 0.620	1.664 0.507
High Rate*	$\bar{x}$ SD	0.042 0.100	0.019 0.041	Tease*	$\bar{x}$ SD	0.028 0.049	0.021 0.032
Humiliate*	$\bar{x}$ SD	0.015 0.019	0.003 0.006	Touch	$\bar{x}$ SD	0.013 0.021	0.020 0.040
Ignore*	$\bar{x}$ SD	0.010 0.013	0.003 0.006	Whine*	$\bar{x}$ SD	0.052 0.074	0.052 0.075
Indulgence	$\bar{x}$ SD	0.000 0.001	0.000 0.000	Work	$\bar{x}$ SD	0.938 0.847	0.958 0.928
Laugh	$\bar{x}$ SD	0.107 0.085	0.160 0.160	Yell*	$\bar{x}$ SD	0.036 0.049	0.025 0.058

* Denotes categories of behavior classed as aversive.

APPENDIX SEVEN

ALL CHILDREN IN FAMILY: BEHAVIOR RATES DURING BASELINE

Behavior		Deviant Families			Normal Families		
		All Children (N=27 families) (N=81 children)	Children 6 yrs & under (N=16 families) (N=22 children)	Children 7 yrs & over (N=23 families) (N=59 children)	All Children (N=27 families) (N=81 children)	Children 6 yrs & under (N=16 families) (N=22 children)	Children 7 yrs & over (N=25 families) (N=59 children)
Total Social Behavior	$\bar{x}$	6.614	6.806	6.768	5.847	6.113	5.761
	SD	1.987	2.192	2.007	1.376	1.329	1.414
Total Deviant Behavior	$\bar{x}$	0.559	0.627	0.517	0.305	0.522	0.242
	SD	0.472	0.482	0.500	0.246	0.366	0.184
Approval	$\bar{x}$	0.014	0.018	0.012	0.028	0.029	0.029
	SD	0.015	0.026	0.015	0.015	0.021	0.018
Attention	$\bar{x}$	1.346	1.605	1.211	1.386	1.708	1.255
	SD	0.481	0.583	0.438	0.490	0.526	0.471
Command	$\bar{x}$	0.051	0.049	0.059	0.038	0.035	0.043
	SD	0.032	0.023	0.049	0.027	0.034	0.031
Command Negative*	$\bar{x}$	0.009	0.007	0.010	0.003	0.003	0.003
	SD	0.013	0.015	0.018	0.004	0.006	0.006
Compliance	$\bar{x}$	0.189	0.278	0.014	0.172	0.237	0.155
	SD	0.138	0.147	0.085	0.118	0.141	0.115
Cry*	$\bar{x}$	0.020	0.047	0.011	0.018	0.041	0.007
	SD	0.032	0.076	0.026	0.037	0.060	0.018
Disapproval*	$\bar{x}$	0.124	0.095	0.142	0.084	0.095	0.088
	SD	0.092	0.079	0.101	0.055	0.081	0.052
Dependency*	$\bar{x}$	0.007	0.012	0.006	0.004	0.006	0.003
	SD	0.014	0.031	0.011	0.007	0.010	0.008
Destructiveness*	$\bar{x}$	0.020	0.015	0.022	0.004	0.007	0.002
	SD	0.039	0.025	0.052	0.006	0.011	0.005
High Rate*	$\bar{x}$	0.042	0.052	0.043	0.017	0.030	0.010
	SD	0.105	0.134	0.111	0.031	0.040	0.026
Humiliate*	$\bar{x}$	0.017	0.007	0.021	0.002	0.003	0.003
	SD	0.024	0.009	0.030	0.004	0.006	0.005
Ignore	$\bar{x}$	0.008	0.004	0.008	0.003	0.002	0.004
	SD	0.010	0.009	0.010	0.006	0.005	0.010
Indulgence	$\bar{x}$	0.000	0.001	0.000	0.000	0.000	0.000
	SD	0.001	0.002	0.000	0.000	0.000	0.000
Laugh	$\bar{x}$	0.098	0.087	0.099	0.139	0.166	0.139
	SD	0.067	0.075	0.066	0.118	0.208	0.108
Non-Compliance*	$\bar{x}$	0.077	0.111	0.054	0.048	0.081	0.038
	SD	0.059	0.076	0.051	0.046	0.061	0.046
Negativism*	$\bar{x}$	0.085	0.059	0.086	0.024	0.014	0.032
	SD	0.105	0.098	0.117	0.028	0.026	0.042
Normative	$\bar{x}$	2.862	2.415	3.013	2.727	2.358	2.737
	SD	0.761	0.619	0.796	0.958	0.833	1.012
No Response	$\bar{x}$	0.071	0.057	0.071	0.057	0.048	0.060
	SD	0.060	0.039	0.064	0.037	0.028	0.043

* Denotes categories of behavior classed as aversive.

APPENDIX SEVEN CONTINUED

ALL CHILDREN IN FAMILY: BEHAVIOR RATES DURING BASELINE

Behavior		Deviant Families			Normal Families		
		All Children (N=27 families) (N=81 children)	Children 6 yrs & under (N=16 families) (N=22 children)	Children 7 yrs & over (N=23 families) (N=59 children)	All Children (N=27 families) (N=81 children)	Children 6 yrs & under (N=16 families) (N=22 children)	Children 7 yrs & over (N=25 families) (N=59 children)
Play	$\bar{x}$	2.066	2.638	1.962	2.437	2.899	2.396
	SD	1.446	1.447	1.388	1.370	1.439	1.429
Physical Negative*	$\bar{x}$	0.028	0.024	0.028	0.012	0.022	0.011
	SD	0.035	0.032	0.038	0.016	0.020	0.018
Physical Positive	$\bar{x}$	0.050	0.061	0.047	0.025	0.040	0.014
	SD	0.091	0.110	0.096	0.032	0.055	0.025
Proximity	$\bar{x}$	0.021	0.038	0.017	0.006	0.017	0.001
	SD	0.042	0.097	0.029	0.031	0.063	0.002
Receive	$\bar{x}$	0.047	0.115	0.025	0.049	0.105	0.024
	SD	0.047	0.111	0.028	0.049	0.073	0.031
Self-Stimulation	$\bar{x}$	0.220	0.227	0.216	0.121	0.225	0.082
	SD	0.185	0.201	0.226	0.125	0.263	0.092
Talk	$\bar{x}$	1.933	1.701	1.930	1.815	1.673	1.869
	SD	0.528	0.672	0.551	0.492	0.507	0.594
Tease*	$\bar{x}$	0.036	0.027	0.035	0.019	0.025	0.020
	SD	0.049	0.062	0.028	0.024	0.038	0.038
Touch	$\bar{x}$	0.015	0.026	0.013	0.017	0.023	0.015
	SD	0.021	0.047	0.018	0.030	0.044	0.023
Whine*	$\bar{x}$	0.043	0.099	0.020	0.045	0.122	0.014
	SD	0.047	0.091	0.025	0.062	0.136	0.023
Work	$\bar{x}$	0.813	0.384	1.046	0.998	0.257	1.245
	SD	0.708	0.802	0.718	0.919	0.235	1.036
Yell*	$\bar{x}$	0.043	0.069	0.032	0.022	0.070	0.007
	SD	0.047	0.106	0.048	0.048	0.153	0.014

* Denotes categories of behavior classed as aversive.

APPENDIX EIGHT

PARENTS: BEHAVIOR RATES DURING BASELINE

Behavior		Deviant Families (N=27)		Normal Families (N=27)	
		Mothers (N=27)	Fathers (N=18)	Mothers (N=27)	Fathers (N=18)
Total Social Behavior	$\bar{x}$	7.087	7.039	6.908	6.487
	SD	2.194	1.617	1.718	1.678
Total Deviant Behavior	$\bar{x}$	0.472	0.285	0.258	0.209
	SD	0.295	0.226	0.185	0.221
Approval	$\bar{x}$	0.050	0.039	0.096	0.108
	SD	0.047	0.039	0.087	0.106
Attention	$\bar{x}$	1.067	1.118	0.986	1.436
	SD	0.478	0.577	0.418	0.635
Command	$\bar{x}$	0.457	0.274	0.392	0.221
	SD	0.254	0.126	0.253	0.141
Command Negative*	$\bar{x}$	0.046	0.023	0.020	0.019
	SD	0.066	0.033	0.039	0.042
Compliance	$\bar{x}$	0.021	0.028	0.016	0.014
	SD	0.024	0.042	0.027	0.016
Cry*	$\bar{x}$	0.000	0.000	0.000	0.000
	SD	0.000	0.000	0.000	0.000
Disapproval*	$\bar{x}$	0.314	0.182	0.183	0.122
	SD	0.193	0.136	0.124	0.134
Dependency*	$\bar{x}$	0.003	0.000	0.000	0.001
	SD	0.013	0.000	0.000	0.003
Destructiveness*	$\bar{x}$	0.000	0.000	0.000	0.000
	SD	0.000	0.000	0.000	0.000
High Rate*	$\bar{x}$	0.000	0.000	0.000	0.000
	SD	0.000	0.000	0.000	0.000
Humiliate*	$\bar{x}$	0.011	0.015	0.001	0.001
	SD	0.022	0.030	0.004	0.004
Ignore	$\bar{x}$	0.023	0.019	0.013	0.002
	SD	0.040	0.023	0.022	0.008
Indulgence	$\bar{x}$	0.014	0.008	0.015	0.021
	SD	0.034	0.018	0.035	0.079
Laugh	$\bar{x}$	0.078	0.062	0.166	0.101
	SD	0.068	0.062	0.125	0.081
Non-Compliance*	$\bar{x}$	0.011	0.009	0.007	0.006
	SD	0.018	0.032	0.012	0.011
Negativism*	$\bar{x}$	0.019	0.012	0.003	0.007
	SD	0.039	0.022	0.008	0.014
Normative	$\bar{x}$	1.629	3.037	1.264	2.923
	SD	1.110	1.032	0.972	1.331
No Response	$\bar{x}$	0.138	0.105	0.109	0.073
	SD	0.072	0.069	0.065	0.048

* Denotes categories of behavior classed as aversive.

APPENDIX EIGHT CONTINUED

PARENTS: BEHAVIOR RATES DURING BASELINE

Behavior		Deviant Families (N=27)		Normal Families (N=27)	
		Mothers (N=27)	Fathers (N=18)	Mothers (N=27)	Fathers (N=18)
Play	$\bar{x}$	0.255	0.715	0.543	0.714
	SD	0.803	1.029	0.711	1.391
Physical Negative*	$\bar{x}$	0.019	0.003	0.007	0.005
	SD	0.045	0.010	0.015	0.017
Physical Positive	$\bar{x}$	0.088	0.092	0.055	0.049
	SD	0.133	0.168	0.073	0.122
Proximity	$\bar{x}$	0.002	0.001	0.001	0.000
	SD	0.007	0.003	0.004	0.000
Receive	$\bar{x}$	0.008	0.020	0.010	0.022
	SD	0.011	0.029	0.017	0.030
Self-Stimulation	$\bar{x}$	0.013	0.026	0.007	0.028
	SD	0.031	0.057	0.014	0.076
Talk	$\bar{x}$	2.966	3.138	3.422	3.087
	SD	0.975	0.986	0.974	1.162
Tease*	$\bar{x}$	0.001	0.014	0.007	0.024
	SD	0.004	0.045	0.015	0.041
Touch	$\bar{x}$	0.051	0.024	0.035	0.020
	SD	0.101	0.040	0.058	0.027
Whine*	$\bar{x}$	0.001	0.000	0.000	0.000
	SD	0.003	0.000	0.000	0.000
Work	$\bar{x}$	3.346	1.277	3.527	1.329
	SD	1.431	1.326	1.722	1.403
Yell*	$\bar{x}$	0.009	0.000	0.001	0.001
	SD	0.019	0.000	0.004	0.002

* Denotes categories of behavior classed as aversive.

APPENDIX NINE

ALL FAMILY MEMBERS: BEHAVIOR RATES DURING BASELINE

Behavior		Deviant Families (N=27) (N=126 members)	Normal Families (N=27) (N=126 Members)	Behavior		Deviant Families (N=27) (N=126 members)	Normal Families (N=27) (N=126 Members)
Total Social Behavior	$\bar{x}$ SD	6.836 1.838	6.163 1.301	Non-Compliance	$\bar{x}$ SD	0.052 0.043	0.032 0.029
Total Deviant Behavior	$\bar{x}$ SD	0.522 0.374	0.276 0.191	Negativism*	$\bar{x}$ SD	0.062 0.075	0.017 0.018
Approval	$\bar{x}$ SD	0.025 0.018	0.056 0.039	Normative	$\bar{x}$ SD	2.622 0.631	2.464 0.729
Attention	$\bar{x}$ SD	1.252 0.331	1.290 0.371	No Response	$\bar{x}$ SD	0.091 0.049	0.072 0.033
Command	$\bar{x}$ SD	0.177 0.090	0.145 0.086	Play	$\bar{x}$ SD	1.399 1.014	1.740 1.044
Command Negative*	$\bar{x}$ SD	0.021 0.026	0.009 0.015	Physical Negative*	$\bar{x}$ SD	0.025 0.033	0.010 0.012
Compliance	$\bar{x}$ SD	0.120 0.070	0.112 0.076	Physical Positive	$\bar{x}$ SD	0.063 0,074	0.033 0.038
Cry*	$\bar{x}$ SD	0.012 0.018	0.010 0.019	Proximity	$\bar{x}$ SD	0.014 0.027	0.004 0.020
Disapproval*	$\bar{x}$ SD	0.181 0.088	0.111 0.065	Receive	$\bar{x}$ SD	0.034 0.027	0.035 0.029
Dependency*	$\bar{x}$ SD	0.005 0.009	0.002 0.004	Self-Stimulation	$\bar{x}$ SD	0.144 0.118	0.081 0.079
Destructiveness*	$\bar{x}$ SD	0.014 0.028	0.002 0.004	Talk	$\bar{x}$ SD	2.355 0.613	2.371 0.602
High Rate*	$\bar{x}$ SD	0.030 0.079	0.011 0.021	Tease*	$\bar{x}$ SD	0.027 0.035	0.016 0.016
Humiliate*	$\bar{x}$ SD	0.017 0.018	0.002 0.003	Touch	$\bar{x}$ SD	0.027 0.038	0.020 0.030
Ignore*	$\bar{x}$ SD	0.013 0.014	0.005 0.007	Whine*	$\bar{x}$ SD	0.027 0.027	0.027 0.036
Indulgence	$\bar{x}$ SD	0.004 0.008	0.007 0.017	Work	$\bar{x}$ SD	1.478 0.623	1.601 0.848
Laugh	$\bar{x}$ SD	0.090 0.052	0.137 0.087	Yell*	$\bar{x}$ SD	0.031 0.033	0.014 0.029

* Denotes categories of behavior classed as aversive.

APPENDIX TEN

DEMOGRAPHIC INFORMATION ON STEALERS, NON-STEALERS, AND NORMALS IN PRESENT SAMPLE (Reid & Hendriks, 1973)

Variable	Normals (N=27)	Stealers (N=14)	Non-Stealers (N=13)
Age of referred child	Mdn = 8 Rng 5-11	Mdn = 8 Rng 5-14	Mdn = 8 Rng 6-11
Number of siblings	Mdn = 3 Rng 2-6	Mdn = 3 Rng 2-6	Mdn = 3 Rng 2-6
Number of families with father absent	9	5	4
Socioeconomic level*	Mdn = 4 Rng 1-7	Mdn = 2nd Rng 2-7	Mdn = 4 Rng 1-6
Birth order of referred child	Mdn = 2nd Rng 1st-6th	Mdn = 2nd Rng 1st-7th	Mdn = 2 Rng 1st-6th
Grades ahead or behind in school for age**	Mdn = 0 Rng - 1 to + 1 year	Mdn = 0 Rng - 1 to + 1 year	Mdn = 0 Rng - 1 to + 1 year

* Based upon system provided by Hollingshead and Redlich (1958) with class 1 denoting higher executive or professional, class 4 clerical and class 7 unskilled laborer.

** No fine-grain data are available on the achievement or intellectual abilities of these children.

APPENDIX ELEVEN

Z SCORES* FOR ORIGINAL DEVIANT CHILD SAMPLE (N=27)

Family	Baseline	Termination	FU1**	FU6**	FU12**
11	1.394	2.166	-0.505	-0.186	-0.505
12	2.028	0.643	0.059	0.076	-0.031
14	1.377	0.830	0.836	2.142	0.680
15	2.054	0.568	0.198	4.305	3.119
16	0.506	1.225	-0.172	0.397	-0.344
17	-0.495	-0.505			
18	6.569	0.624	6.548		
21	0.724	-0.371	-0.225		
22	-0.148	-0.392	-0.119	-0.255	-0.451
24	0.969	0.195	-0.214	-0.416	1.693
25	3.213	6.121	1.064	0.114	
26	1.605	1.450			
27	0.729	0.005	-0.025	0.943	0.233
28	-0.011	0.923	1.807	2.047	0.774
29	-0.452	-0.441			
31	0.547	-0.224	-0.290	0.884	-0.255
32	-0.036	-0.451			
33	-0.266	-0.281	1.738	-0.322	1.462
35	-0.228	2.304	0.512	0.641	0.036
36	0.284	1.014	-0.194	0656	2.530
38	0.032	0.069	1.671		-0.142
39	0.033	-0.081	1.400	-0.041	-0.350
40	0.678	0.019	5.269	-0.326	-0.398
42	-0.241	0.584		0.613	
43	2.874	1.723			
44	8.295	0.856	-0.001	0.858	
45	10.513	3.118	4.061		

*Standardized using matched sample of normals.
** FU = Follow-up in months after termination.

APPENDIX TWELVE

Z-Scores for Coercive Behaviors (Rate Per Minute)*

Z	CN	CR	DI	DP	DS	HR	HU	IG	NC	NE	PN	TE	WH	YE
10.0	0.052	0.122	0.754	0.083	0.126	0.414	0.041	0.094	0.610	0.325	0.229	0.380	1.209	0.808
9.8	.051	.120	.741	.081	.124	.406	.040	.092	.599	.319	.225	.373	.186	.729
9.6	.050	.117	.727	.080	.121	.398	.039	.090	.588	.313	.220	.366	.162	.776
9.4	.049	.115	.714	.078	.119	.390	.039	.089	.576	.307	.216	.358	.139	.761
9.2	.048	.112	.700	.077	.116	.382	.038	.087	.565	.301	.211	.351	.115	.745
9.0	.047	.110	.687	.075	.114	.374	.037	.085	.554	.295	.207	.344	.092	.729
8.8	.046	.108	.674	.073	.112	.366	.036	.083	.543	.289	.203	.337	.069	.713
8.6	.045	.105	.660	.072	.109	.358	.035	.081	.532	.283	.198	.330	.045	.697
8.4	.044	.103	.647	.070	.107	.350	.035	.080	.520	.277	.194	.322	.022	.682
8.2	.043	.100	.633	.069	.104	.342	.034	.078	.509	.271	.189	.315	.998	.666
8.0	.042	.098	.620	.067	.102	.334	.033	.076	.498	.265	.185	.308	.975	.650
7.8	.041	.096	.607	.065	.100	.326	.032	.074	.487	.259	.181	.301	.952	.634
7.6	.040	.093	.593	.064	.097	.318	.031	.072	.476	.253	.176	.294	.928	.618
7.4	.039	.091	.580	.062	.095	.310	.031	.071	.464	.247	.172	.286	.905	.603
7.2	.038	.088	.566	.061	.092	.302	.030	.069	.453	.241	.167	.279	.881	.587
7.0	.037	.086	.553	.059	.090	.294	.029	.067	.447	.235	.163	.272	.858	.571
6.8	.036	.084	.540	.057	.088	.286	.028	.065	.431	.229	.159	.265	.835	.555
6.6	.035	.081	.526	.056	.085	.278	.027	.063	.420	.223	.154	.253	.811	.539
6.4	.034	.079	.513	.054	.083	.270	.027	.062	.408	.217	.150	.250	.788	.524
6.2	.033	.076	.499	.053	.080	.262	.026	.060	.397	.211	.145	.243	.764	.508
6.0	.032	.074	.486	.051	.078	.254	.025	.058	.386	.205	.141	.236	.741	.492
5.8	.031	.072	.474	.050	.076	.247	.024	.056	.376	.200	.137	.230	.720	.478
5.6	.030	.069	.459	.048	.073	.238	.023	.054	.364	.193	.132	.222	.694	.460
5.4	.029	.067	.446	.046	.071	.230	.023	.053	.352	.187	.128	.214	.671	.445
5.2	.028	.064	.432	.045	.068	.222	.022	.051	.341	.181	.123	.207	.647	.429
5.0	.027	.062	.419	.043	.066	.214	.021	.049	.330	.175	.119	.200	.624	.413
4.8	.026	.060	.406	.041	.064	.206	.020	.047	.319	.169	.115	.193	.601	.397
4.6	.025	.057	.392	.040	.061	.198	.019	.045	.308	.163	.110	.186	.577	.381
4.4	.024	.055	.379	.038	.059	.190	.019	.044	.296	.157	.106	.178	.554	.366
4.2	.023	.052	.365	.037	.056	.182	.018	.042	.285	.151	.101	.171	.530	.350
4.0	.022	.050	.352	.035	.054	.174	.017	.040	.274	.145	.097	.164	.507	.334
3.8	.021	.048	.339	.033	.052	.166	.016	.038	.263	.139	.093	.157	.484	.318
3.6	.020	.045	.325	.032	.049	.158	.015	.036	.252	.133	.088	.150	.460	.302
3.4	.019	.043	.312	.030	.047	.150	.015	.035	.240	.127	.084	.142	.437	.287
3.2	.018	.040	.298	.029	.044	.142	.014	.033	.229	.121	.079	.135	.413	.271
3.0	.017	.038	.285	.027	.042	.134	.013	.031	.218	.115	.075	.128	.390	.255
2.8	.016	.036	.272	.025	.040	.126	.012	.029	.207	.109	.071	.121	.367	.239
2.6	.015	.033	.258	.024	.037	.118	.011	.027	.196	.103	.066	.114	.343	.223
2.4	.014	.031	.245	.022	.035	.110	.011	.026	.184	.097	.062	.106	.320	.208
2.2	.013	.028	.231	.021	.032	.102	.010	.024	.173	.091	.057	.099	.296	.192
2.0	.012	.026	.218	.019	.030	.094	.009	.022	.162	.085	.053	.092	.273	.176
1.8	.011	.024	.205	.017	.028	.086	.008	.020	.151	.079	.049	.085	.250	.160
1.6	.010	.021	.191	.016	.025	.078	.007	.018	.140	.073	.044	.078	.226	.144
1.4	.009	.019	.178	.014	.023	.070	.007	.017	.128	.067	.040	.070	.203	.129
1.2	.008	.016	.164	.013	.020	.062	.006	.015	.117	.061	.035	.063	.179	.113
1.0	.007	.014	.151	.011	.018	.054	.005	.013	.106	.055	.031	.056	.156	.097
0.8	.006	.012	.138	.009	.016	.046	.004	.011	.095	.049	.027	.049	.133	.081
0.6	.005	.009	.124	.008	.013	.038	.003	.009	.084	.043	.022	.042	.109	.065
0.4	.004	.007	.111	.006	.011	.030	.003	.008	.072	.037	.018	.034	.086	.050
0.2	.003	.004	.097	.005	.008	.022	.002	.006	.061	.031	.013	.027	.062	.034
0.0	.002	.002	.084	.003	.006	.014	.001	.004	.050	.025	.009	.020	.039	.018
−0.2	.001	.000	.071	.001	.004	.006	.000	.002	.039	.019	.005	.013	.016	.002
−0.4	.000		.057	.000	.001	.000		.000	.028	.013	.000	.006	.000	.000
−0.6			.044		.000				.016	.007		.001		
−0.8			.030						.005	.001		.000		
−1.0			.017						.000	.000				
−1.2			.004											
−1.4			.000											
S.D.	.005	.012	.067	.008	.012	.040	.004	.009	.055	.030	.022	.036	.116	.079

*These data are based upon six to ten observation sessions in the homes of 27 non-problem children. The distributions for the 81 children in these families were analyzed separately for boys (N=52) and girls (N=29) and/or children above (N=59) and below (N=22) the ages of six years.

From Patterson, Reid, Jones, and Patterson (1975).

APPENDIX THIRTEEN

OBSERVER RELIABILITY: PERCENT AGREEMENT
(ENTRY X ENTRY) AND CORRELATION (ACROSS PROTOCOLS)*
on 29 Behavioral Categories in the Family Interaction Coding System (FICS).

Code	Rxy	% Agree
Ap	.76	54
At	.96	90
Cm	.93	86
Cn	.66	65
Cr.	.96	72
Di	.92	72
Dp	.88	91
Ds	.92	75
Hr	.65	59
Hu	.92	74
Lg	.93	68
In	.86	61
La	.96	74
Nc	.67	61
Ne	.59	38
No	.99	95
Nr	.95	96
Pl	1.00	75
Pn	.94	57
Pp	.73	59
Px	Not Observed	--
Rc	.89	59
Ss	.67	30
Ta	.99	94
Te	.86	56
Th	.88	91
Wh	.71	49
Wk	.94	92
Ye	.80	56

*Based on analysis of 11 protocols.